Catholic Study Guides for Mary Fabyan Windeatt's

Saint Thomas Aquinas,
The Story of "The Dumb Ox"

Patron Saint of First Communicants,
The Story of Blessed Imelda Lambertini

Saint Catherine of Siena,
The Story of the Girl Who Saw Saints in the Sky

The Miraculous Medal,
The Story of Our Lady's Appearances to
Saint Catherine Labouré

RACE for Heaven's Grades 3-4 Study Guides

Janet P. McKenzie

Biblio Resource Publications, Inc.
Bessemer, Michigan

St. Thomas Aquinas Study Guide © 2001 by Janet P. McKenzie
The Patron Saint of First Communicants Study Guide © 2001 by Janet P. McKenzie
St. Catherine of Siena Study Guide © 2001 by Janet P. McKenzie
The Miraculous Medal Study Guide © 2003 by Janet P. McKenzie

Catholic Study Guides for Mary Fabyan Windeatt's Saints Grades 3 and 4 © 2007 by Janet P. McKenzie

ISBN 978-1-934185-06-3
Second printing 2012

Published by Biblio Resource Publications, Inc.
108 ½ South Moore Street
Bessemer, MI 49911
info@BiblioResource.com
www.BiblioResource.com

A **R**ead **A**loud **C**urriculum **E**nrichment Product
www.RACEforHeaven.com

Cover photo of Obelisk and Basilica in St. Peters Square, Rome © iofoto - Fotolia.com

Special thanks to Julia Fogassy from Our Father's House for her editorial assistance

All quotations from the Windeatt biographies are excerpted from the edition published by Tan Books and Publisher, Inc. If using the original hardback version of these books, note that the text will be the same but the page numbers will vary from the Tan edition.

Printed in the United States of America

Table of Contents

Spiritual Read Aloud

Spiritual Reading

In *My Daily Bread, A Summary of the Spiritual Life* by Father Anthony Paone, S.J., Christ tells us,

> My Child, reading and reflecting are a great help to your spiritual life. My doctrine is explained in many books. . . . Some of these books are written simply, and some are very profound and learned. Choose those which will help you most toward a greater understanding and appreciation of My Truth. Do not read to impress others but rather to be impressed yourself. Read so that you may learn My way of thinking and of doing things.

In her book, *Saint Dominic, Preacher of the Rosary and Founder of the Dominican Order*, Mary Fabyan Windeatt quotes St. Dominic as saying, "A little good reading, much prayer and meditation . . . and God will do the rest." Father Peter-Thomas Rohrbach, O.C.D., states that spiritual reading is the "third essential asset for mediation" (after detachment and recollection). The great value he places on the habit of spiritual reading is expressed in his book *Conversation with Christ, An Introduction to Mental Prayer*:

> We live in a world devoid, in great part, of a Christian spirit, in an atmosphere and culture estranged from God. Living in such a non-theological environment makes it difficult for us to remain in contact with the person of Christ and the true purpose of life itself. We must, if we are to remain realistically attached to Christ, combat this atmosphere and surround ourselves with a new one. Constant spiritual reading fills our minds with Christ and His doctrine—it creates this new climate for us.
>
> In former ages, spiritual reading was not as essential for one's prayer life. People lived in a Christian world and culture which was reflected in their laws, customs, amusements, and their very outlook on life. This situation has radically altered in the last two hundred years, and men must now compensate for this deficit through other media, principally reading. And as the de-Christianization of our world continues, the necessity for spiritual reading simultaneously increases. We stand in need of something to bridge the gap between our pagan surroundings and our conversation with Christ—spiritual reading fills this need.
>
> There is today in our country an alarming decline in general reading of all types. It has been estimated that in 1955 an astonishing forty-eight percent of the American adult population reads *no books at all*, and only eighteen percent read from one to four books. The decline in reading is naturally reflected in religious reading as well. And, while the lack of secular reading will occasion a decrease in culture life, the decline in religious reading

will have repercussions of a more serious nature—severe detriment to one's spiritual life. Any serious attempt to better one's life spiritually should, therefore, include the resolution to engage in more spiritual reading.

If we confine our reading to non-Catholic books, magazines and newspapers, we almost automatically exclude ourselves from full development in our prayer life. The maxims and philosophy of life expressed in these avenues of communication slowly begin to seep into our lives until eventually they occupy a ruling position. We will not have surrounded ourselves with a new climate; rather, the non-Catholic climate will have engulfed us (Chapter 19).

As this decry of the "de-Christianization of our world" was written in 1956, one can safely surmise that the necessity of cultivating the habit of spiritual reading can only have grown in the past several decades.

Spiritual Read Aloud

As supported above, spiritual reading is an essential element of every Christian's life. However, as demonstrated by the ancient practice within monasteries of spiritual read-aloud, this habit is a powerful tool for shared community growth in the spiritual life. For Catholic families, the practice of reading spiritual books aloud produces four desirable effects:

I.   It reinforces the habit of spiritual reading for each member of the family and allows each member to practice this habit regardless of age.

II.   It reinforces the habit of spiritual conversation if the reading results in even a general discussion of the values and virtues being portrayed in the story.

III. It strengthens the family as the domestic Church where members exist to learn and live the Faith together for the support and enrichment of all family members.

IV.   It allows the discussion and demonstration of the practical application of the Faith for all age levels.

The Habit of Spiritual Reading

As outlined above, establishing the habit of daily spiritual reading is essential to our spiritual growth. Through read-aloud, children can be taught at an early age that daily spiritual reading is a fun, rewarding exercise. Do make this time together pleasant by allowing the children to do crafts, draw, play quietly with puzzles, toys, etc. As long as their attention is not divided and they can participate in a discussion of the reading afterwards, allow quiet activity. One cannot expect children to sit piously with hands clasped prayerfully throughout the read-aloud session! As the children get older, encourage them to read other spiritual books, including the Bible, during a quiet time of their own. Model this habit by allowing them to observe your habit of daily spiritual reading as well. Although the family read-aloud sessions may be as long as thirty minutes, private spiritual reading times may be considerably shorter depending on the habits and temperament of each child.

The Habit of Spiritual Conversation
This habit, for many families, may begin with spiritual read-aloud. When each member of the family participates in a spiritual discussion of a religious book, the practice of discussing matters of faith and Christ-like living begins to form. If the formation of holy habits and imitation of the saints is the goal, these discussions will become common-place in the home as each member checks the others on their actions and words. As family members become more comfortable and open about spiritual matters, this practice will soon spread into other areas of their lives. Spiritual discussions with friends and other relatives will become more natural and in fact become important topics to be discussed. Sharing one's own spirituality and encouraging others to become more open about matters of faith will then become an integral pattern of living.

Strengthening the Domestic Church
As we read more about the saints and their lives and begin to share our faith more openly with others, we realize the importance of holy companionship—living with others who share our faith ideas and supporting each other in our attempts to become more like Christ. Families begin to growth together in their knowledge of the Catholic faith and become more willing to support each other throughout the ups and downs of com-munity living. We begin to "bear one another's burdens with peace and harmony and unselfishness." Just as Christ has His Church to help bring salvation to all, we—as family members—have each other to provide mutual support and encouragement in our efforts to enter the narrow gate. Within our families, we can create the Catholic culture that is missing from our world's culture.

The Practical Application of the Faith for All Age Levels
When lives of the saints are read aloud in the family setting, all aged children can partic-ipate in a discussion of the imitation of the saint's virtues and holy habits. Each member can help others understand how to apply the lessons the saints teach us on a practical level. All family members can help choose a particular habit or virtue upon which to focus. A reward system can be established for virtuous behavior. A family "plan of attack" on non-virtuous habits and attitudes can be developed, implemented, checked, and revised. All members can be encouraged and taught to imitate Christ by the imita-tion of His saints.

Summary
Regular family read-loud sessions that center around the lives of the saints will benefit the family with an increased interest in reading—especially saintly literature, a growth in vocabulary, and an improved sense of family unity. Additionally, family members will be encouraged to develop the habit of spiritual reading on their own, will become more comfortable and experienced with spiritual conversation, and be able to apply the Truths of the Catholic faith, on a practical level, to all aspects of their lives—no matter what their age. The customs, habits, and attitudes of the family will more and more reflect those of the Catholic culture. Perseverance in this simple daily ritual will help to "bridge the gap between our pagan surroundings and our conversation with Christ."

When Mother Reads Aloud

When Mother reads aloud the past
Seems real as every day;
I hear the tramp of armies vast,
I see the spears and lances cast,
I join the thrilling fray;
Brave knights and ladies fair and proud
I meet when Mother reads aloud.

When Mother reads aloud, far lands
Seem very near and true;
I cross the desert's gleaming sands,
Or hunt the jungle's prowling bands,
Or sail the ocean blue;

Far heights, whose peaks the cold mists
    shroud,
I scale, when Mother reads aloud.

When Mother reads aloud I long
For noble deeds to do—
To help the right, redress the wrong,
It seems so easy to be strong, so simple
    to be true,
O, thick and fast the visions crowd
When Mother reads aloud.
                    —*Anonymous*

The Reading Mother

I had a mother who read to me
Sagas of pirates who scoured the sea,
Cutlasses clenched in their yellow teeth,
"Blackbirds" stowed in the hold beneath.

I had a mother who read me plays
Of ancient and gallant and golden days
Stories of Marmion and Ivanhoe,
Which every boy has a right to know.

I had a mother who read me tales
Of Gelert, the hound of the hills of
  Wales,

True to his trust till his tragic death,
Faithfulness blest with his final breath.

I had a mother who read me things
That wholesome life to the boy-heart
    brings—
Stories that stir with an upward touch,
O, that each mother of boys were such.

You may have tangible wealth untold,
Caskets of jewels and coffers of gold.
Richer than I you can never be—
I had a mother who read to me.
                    —*Strickland Gullilan*

How to Use These Study Guides

A Word about Grade Level Work

These four books—*Saint Thomas Aquinas, Patron Saint of First Communicants, Saint Catherine,* and *The Miraculous Medal*—have been selected for the Grades 3-4 series as these books are the shortest in length of any of the Windeatt saint biographies. However, the activities within each study guide are designed for varying grade levels. Some activities, therefore, will be too difficult for third and fourth grade students to complete on their own. Use discretion when proceeding through the various exercises. Utilize only those activities that are appropriate for each student.

✖REVIEW✖ Vocabulary

Vocabulary words are listed at the beginning of each lesson. Words on the left are secular words and are given within the sentence structure. Allow students to guess the meaning of the italicized word before looking it up. This helps them to surmise the meaning from context, a skill that enhances reading comprehension and strengthens vocabulary. Vocabulary words listed in the right-hand column are Catholic vocabulary words. Help students identify any suffixes, prefixes or root words that might give clues to the word's meaning. To help with definitions and proper usage, use a dictionary. For Catholic vocabulary words, use a Catholic encyclopedia, dictionary, or catechism.

??? Comprehension Questions/Narration Prompts

These questions are appropriate for all age levels. They can be used several ways, depending on a student's ability. For students with difficulty in reading comprehension, read and briefly discuss these questions before reading the chapter. Discuss, too, the sub-title provided under each chapter heading in the study guide. The student will then know what content to watch for within the reading. If read afterward, the questions become a *test of,* rather than an *aid to,* comprehension. For students with adequate comprehension skills, use the questions for oral review after the reading to insure that important content has been absorbed.

Use these questions too as prompts for narration, which is simply the oral retelling of the story in the student's own words. It is a helpful tool to determine the level of each student's comprehension. All ages may benefit from the practice of narration. If done within a mixed age group, begin with the youngest students and have the older students add details to the already-related story.

Answers to comprehension questions are provided in the answer key.

Forming Opinions/Drawing Conclusions

More than relating events, these questions require the student to develop an opinion, or to uncover or discover material not expressly stated in the text. They are designed to develop thinking skills and do not usually require the use of any outside resources. Use this section with children grades five and up as the basis for discussion or as a writing assignment.

For Further Study

Appropriate for upper elementary through high school grades, this section requires the use of additional reference materials. These activities invite students to look more deeply at the historical events and people that shaped the times of each character. Topics in this section may be used for honing research skills, or for oral presentations and/or written reports.

Growing in Holiness

These activities are different from the others in that they do not involve discussion or study as much as personal action and interior reflection. They can perhaps be considered "conversion activities" or "life lessons." By applying the spiritual lessons of the story to everyday life, the student is encouraged to develop habits in imitation of the saints—which is an imitation of Christ Himself. Remember to reinforce these activities with the student and to comment when they are observed in action.

Geography

The map provided with this study guide serves to orient the students with respect to space—*where* the action of the story is taking place—as well as to acquaint them with common geographical landmarks. Permission is hereby granted to photocopy maps for family or classroom use.

Timeline Work

The creation of a timeline allows students to place the story's events within a wider historical framework. Simple directions for making a timeline are included in the study guide. Students will need plain paper, colored markers, and a ruler.

✓ Checking the Catechism

For older students, these activities require a copy of the *Catechism of the Catholic Church* (*CCC*) or its *Compendium*. The references for the more concise *Compendium* appear in parentheses after the *CCC* citations. Older students can read aloud—and then discuss—the stated text paragraphs with an adult.

For younger students, use any grade-appropriate catechism to review the doctrines and terms as specified. An excellent activity book for multi-grades is Ignatius Press' *100 Activities Based on the Catechism of the Catholic Church* by Ellen Rossini. Discuss together how the specific topics from the catechism are illustrated in the thoughts and actions of the characters in the book.

Searching Scripture

Familiarize the student with the inspired Word of God by studying the biblical passages provided. Strengthen these exercises by occasionally requiring memorization of the verse(s). Stress that knowledge of Scripture is an important part of our faith education.

Note that Ms. Windeatt used the Douay-Rheims translation of the Bible, which was the translation in use in the United States until 1970 when it was replaced by the New American Bible in the *Lectionary of Mass*. The Douay-Rheims translation is taken from the Latin Vulgate, whereas the New American translation comes from the original languages of Hebrew, Aramaic or Greek (as the case may be for each specific book). For this reason, some of the books' names (as well as some of the Psalms' numbers) differ between these two translations. When these differences occur in the biblical citiations within this study guide, the New American references are given first with the Douay-Rheims references following in parentheses. All biblical references used in this study guide are from the New American translation.

Test

The purpose of the test is to ensure that the student has comprehended the important events in each saint's life as well as the lessons the story intends to impart. An answer key is provided for these questions.

In addition to the test, many students will benefit from the completion of a book report. See RACE for Heaven's *Alternative Book Reports for Catholic Students* for additional information on book reports specifically geared toward saint biographies. Consider requiring each student to choose one of these reports or activities upon completion of the Windeatt biography.

Warning

These study guides are comprehensive. They contain activities for a variety of age levels and areas of study. Do **not** attempt to complete every activity for every lesson. Do only those exercises that are suitable for the needs of your current situation. Resist the impulse to be so thorough that the story line of the book is lost, and the read-aloud sessions become dreaded rather than anticipated. The activities are designed to enhance your reading—not to become the dictating tyrant of your read-aloud time together. If you are using these guides for young audiences, consider just using the comprehension and opinion questions as well as the "Growing in Holiness" section; use the maps as a geographical visual aid. Re-read the books to complete the more advanced activities in later years.

Another suggestion is to use the activities designed for older students in coordination with their history, geography, writing and/or religious curriculum. Each study guide could also be used as a complete unit study for hectic times when regular school may not be in session such as Advent, times of family stress (the birth of a new sibling, for example) or over the summer months. In reading the book and completing the activities, subjects such as religion, reading, writing, geography, and history can all be easily covered.

The most important rules to the successful use of these enrichment activities are
1. Be creative rather than obsessive.
2. Be flexible rather than overly structured.
3. Enjoy!

Study Guide for

Saint Thomas Aquinas,
The Story of "The Dumb Ox"

St. Thomas Aquinas

St. Thomas Aquinas was called the "Dumb Ox"
Though it appears he was smart as a fox.
The things he did think
Were really in sync
With thoughts that the Holy Spirit unlocks.

To Monte Cassino his father did send,
The Benedictines to Thomas he did recommend.
Tom learned quite a lot,
So much that they sought
To send him to college—Naples did attend.

Then Thomas met up with the friars in white.
When he tried to join them, his family did fight.
They sent him to prison
In tower arisen
Till dropped in a basket in mid of the night.

Then to the Dominicans he did profess
And in their white habit, he proudly did dress.
He kept up his learning—
Midnight oil burning—
Till doctorate standing he came to possess.

He read from the Bible, knew most of the Book,
Had crucifix hanging from 'most every nook.
Some hymns he did write
But then caught a sight,
A vision of heaven and how it did look.

The feast of the Body and Blood of our Lord,
We owe to Saint Thomas because he explored
The need to observe—
Indeed to reserve—
A day to commemorate He who's adored.

Think what you can learn from this saint and his tale.
How you can apply it to help you prevail.
Then mold what you do
And boldly pursue
His pattern of holiness. Follow his trail.

Timeline of Events

Year	Event
1119	University of Bologna founded
1150	University of Paris founded
1152-1190	Frederick I emperor of Rome (Thomas' father's uncle)
1193	Birth of St. Albert the Great (died 1280)
1194-1260	Erection of Chartres Cathedral
1200	Cambridge University founded
1202-1204	Fourth Crusade; University of Siena and University of Vicenza founded
1206-1227	Genghis Khan chief prince of Mongols
1209	St. Francis establishes the first Franciscan rule
1212	Children's Crusade
1214	Birth of Roger Bacon, Franciscan monk and English philosopher (died 1294)
1215	Magna Charta signed by King John of England, Fourth Lateran Council
1217	University of Salamanca founded
1224-1229	Founding of University of Naples and Toulouse University
1225	Birth of Thomas Aquinas
1228	St. Francis canonized
1230	Wenceslas, King of Bohemia (until 1253)
1231	Thomas begins school at Monte Cassino; Papal Inquisition begins
1243	Thomas joins the Dominican Order
1246	Thomas begins his study under Albert the Great
1247	First Council of Lyons
1249-1250	Oxford University founded; four colleges established at University of Paris
1250	Thomas ordained a priest
1251	Simon Stock sees vision of our Lady and is given the Brown Scapular
1256	Beginning of the Hundred Years' War between Venice and Genoa
1257	Thomas received the degree of Doctor of Theology
1259	Kublai Khan rules Mongol Empire
1264	Thomas writes *Summa Contra Gentiles,* begins his prayers to the Blessed Sacrament in anticipation of the Feast of Corpus Christi, begins writing *Summa Theologica*
1267	Aztecs found Tenochtitlan (Mexico City)
1268-1271	Three year vacancy in the papacy
1270	Marco Polo journeys to China
1274	Death of Thomas; canonized in 1323; declared Doctor of Church in 1567; Second Council of Lyons
1275-1271	Marco Polo in the service of Kublai Khan
1276	Year of four popes
1289-1290	Founding of University of Montpelier (France) and University of Lisbon
1303-1309	Founding of the University of Rome and University of Orleans
1338-1340	Founding of University of Pisa and University of Grenoble

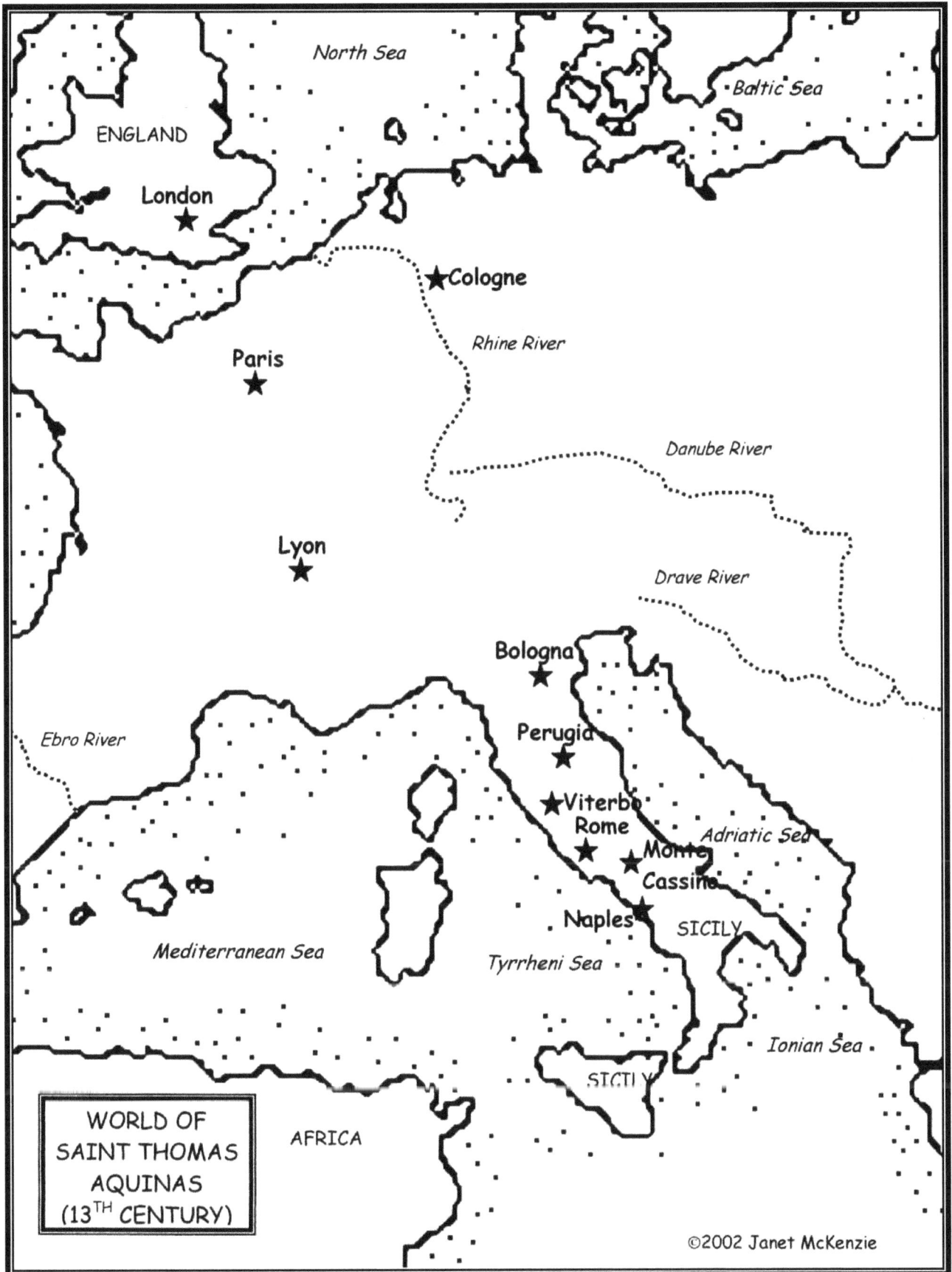

North Sea

ENGLAND

London

Baltic Sea

★Cologne

Rhine River

Paris

Danube River

Lyon

Drave River

Bologna

Ebro River

Perugia

★Viterbo
Rome

Adriatic Sea

Monte
Cassine

Naples

SICILY

Mediterranean Sea

Tyrrheni Sea

Ionian Sea

SICILY

AFRICA

WORLD OF
SAINT THOMAS
AQUINAS
(13TH CENTURY)

©2002 Janet McKenzie

Introduction–In Which Thomas Tells Us of His Patronage

★REVIEW★ Vocabulary
made me *Patron* of Catholic Schools   *Dominican*
special *charge* of each Catholic student   *Pope*

??? Comprehension Questions/Narration Prompts
1. What did Thomas feel is the least important part of a person?
2. Refer to page 76 of the Windeatt biography to determine exactly what year St. Thomas Aquinas was declared the Patron Saint of Catholic Schools as well as Patron Saint of all universities and colleges.

Forming Opinions/Drawing Conclusions
1. Thomas Aquinas was born in 1225; about how old was he when he died?
2. State why you believe St. Thomas Aquinas was declared the Patron Saint of Catholic Schools. Refer to the Declaration of Pope Leo XIII on page 76 in the Windeatt biography for additional information.

For Further Study
1. In Pope Leo XIII's Declaration on page 76, he refers to St. Thomas Aquinas as the "Angelic Doctor." Research "Doctor of the Church" in a Catholic dictionary. What is necessary to be proclaimed a Doctor of the Church? Why do you think St. Thomas Aquinas was given this honor? (See page 56 below for a complete list of the Doctors of the Catholic Church. Who is the most recent Doctor of the Church?)
2. Read more about patron saints on page 13 below.

✝ Growing in Holiness
Remember to pray to St. Thomas daily and ask for his help in your studies, especially your most difficult subject. You may also wish to ask him to help you as you read this book, so you may thoroughly understand his life and the lessons it can teach.

✓ Checking the Catechism
As a patron and a saint, Thomas asks you to think of him as your friend. Older students may read text paragraphs 954-963 (194-195) in the *Catechism of the Catholic Church* (*CCC*) on "The Communion of the Church of Heaven and Earth." Younger students should review the communion of saints, honoring the saints, and the intercession of the saints in their own catechisms. If desired, complete Activity #80 in *100 Activities Based on the Catechism of the Catholic Church* (*100 Activities*).

Chapter 1–In Which Thomas Goes to School

⟨REVIEW⟩ Vocabulary

I answered *meekly*	*Benedictine*
put in Theodora *wistfully*	*Abbot*

??? Comprehension Questions/Narration Prompts

1. How old was Thomas when he was sent away to boarding school?
2. Under what religious order was the abbey of Monte Cassino? Who was the founder of this order? What was their most important work?

Forming Opinions/Drawing Conclusions

1. Discuss how Thomas must have felt as a six-year-old boy living away from home. Remember that he did not see his family again until five years later.
2. Explain which activities of the monks at the Benedictine monastery reflected the motto of its founder, St. Benedict: *Ora et labora* (Pray and work).

For Further Study

Research Frederick Barbarossa (Red Beard), who was also known as Frederick I, including his role in the Third Crusade. Frederick was the Emperor of the Holy Roman Empire from 1152 to 1190. Thomas' father was his nephew.

Growing in Holiness

Listen to a recording of Gregorian chant. If this is not possible, try to find a copy of the prayer book for the Liturgy of the Hours (Divine Office). Read some of the Psalms that are read each day. Notice the various hours that the monks would gather to pray. Try to read a psalm every third hour throughout the day. Read Psalm 120 (119):164.

Timeline Work

Taping sheets of plain paper end-to-end, make a timeline representing the years from 1119 through 1340. Let three inches equal 25 years. Mark on your timeline the dates and events from 1119 through 1231, using information from page 2.

✓ Checking the Catechism

Older students may read text paragraph 2834 in the *CCC* on Christian prayer and the motto of St. Benedict.

Chapter 2—In Which Thomas Goes to Naples

✖ᴿᴱⱽᴵᴱᵂ Vocabulary

thieves and *ruffians* who lurked   *convent*
happy *repose* of Father's soul   *founder*

⁇⁇ Comprehension Questions/Narration Prompts

1. What gifts did God give to Thomas?
2. What two aspects of the Dominican life attracted Thomas?

💡 Forming Opinions/Drawing Conclusions

Try to predict what kind of "fuss" there will be when Thomas' family hears of his decision to join the Dominican order. Remember Thomas' allusion to "poor Father" and his family's expectations of him regarding the Benedictine Abbey of Monte Cassino. (If you need a hint, read the title of the next chapter.)

📖 For Further Study

St. Dominic de Guzman was canonized a saint in 1234, only thirteen years after his death and during the lifetime of St. Thomas Aquinas (1225-1274). St. Francis of Assisi lived from 1181-1226. Both the Dominican and Franciscan orders were relatively new during St. Thomas' life. Compare and contrast the orders established by Sts. Benedict, Dominic, and Francis. What was the primary purpose for which each order was founded?

✠ Growing in Holiness

Thomas talks about the students "paying a visit" to a church. Sometime this week try to visit Jesus in the tabernacle at a church near you. Offer your prayers there for a Holy Soul in Purgatory—perhaps the soul of someone who has recently died. If you are unable to go to church, send your guardian angel to keep Jesus company there for you.

🗺 Geography

Trace and label the map found on page 3. Draw a line from Monte Cassino to Naples to indicate Thomas' move there. As the story continues, draw lines to represent the travels of St. Thomas; draw each chapter in different colors. Keep in mind that Thomas (like most people of his day) usually traveled by foot or horseback. On a modern map, find the names of the countries in which these cities are now located.

Chapter 3–In Which Thomas Goes to Prison

⟪REVIEW⟫ Vocabulary

danger of your mother's *wrath*   *Master General*
to *taunt* me for being a fool   *Eternal City*

⁇⁇ Comprehension Questions/Narration Prompts

1. Why did Thomas go to Paris?
2. Name three reasons why Thomas' mother did not approve of him becoming a Dominican. What did his family do to get Thomas to give up his Dominican habit?
3. How did Thomas scare the girl out of the tower?

💡 Forming Opinions/Drawing Conclusions

1. On page 28, Thomas states, "If Father were alive, he would have been thoroughly ashamed of me." What might have happened differently in Thomas' life if his father had still been alive at this time? Explain why Thomas' mother believed it necessary to imprison him. Try to see the situation as she would see it—as head of the household trying to enforce what she believed to be her deceased husband's wishes.
2. What sacrifices did Thomas have to make in order to pursue his religious vocation? What might you have done given similar circumstances? In your own words, state what it means to discern and follow your religious vocation. (See pages 28-29 for Thomas' description.)

✠ Growing in Holiness

Thomas is knocked to the ground, his hands are tied, and he is placed on a horse; he is then taken against his will to his family's castle—what he calls a "tiresome journey" (page 26). Only when the castle is in view, does Thomas speak of anger—he speaks of how he can scarcely keep the anger out of his heart. The next time you are tempted to anger when mistreated by a brother, sister or friend, remember how poorly Thomas was treated, and yet how controlled his anger was. Ask for the grace to imitate St. Thomas.

✓ Checking the Catechism

Sins against the fourth, fifth, and sixth commandments are apparent in this chapter. Older students may read in the *CCC* text paragraph 2067 (455, 464, 470, and 487-492) as well as the summary of the commandments found before text paragraph 2052 while younger students review the fourth through sixth commandments in their own catechisms. Find references to sins against these commandments—as well as how characters honored these commandments—in this chapter. If desired, use Activity #16 in *100 Activities* to review the Ten Commandments.

Chapter 4–In Which Thomas Goes to Cologne

Vocabulary

Were my sisters *deceiving* me   *Profession*
a certain problem in *theology*   *Vatican*

Comprehension Questions/Narration Prompts
1. What gift did God give Thomas as a reward for persevering in his religious vocation?
2. How did Thomas escape from the tower? How long had he been a prisoner there? How did Thomas spend much of his time during his imprisonment in the tower?

Forming Opinions/Drawing Conclusions
Give an explanation for Thomas' nickname, "The Dumb Ox of Sicily." (See the answer key below if assistance is needed.)

For Further Study
Research the life of St. Albert the Great of Cologne (another Doctor of the Church), who lived from 1206 to 1280.

Growing in Holiness
Thomas knew the Bible very well and, in fact, had most of it memorized. Resolve to read the Bible for fifteen minutes each day. Begin with the New Testament and the Psalms. Choose a psalm, and memorize it.

(Note: The Bible translation used in the United States at the time of Ms. Windeatt's writing was the Douay-Rheims. The New American translation, printed in 1970, combines Psalms 9 and 10 of both the Latin Vulgate of St. Jerome—which was the Bible translation in use during the lifetime of St. Thomas—and the Douay-Rheims translation, which was first published in 1609. This means that the psalm chapter referred to by Ms. Windeatt would not be the same chapter in a New American Bible. If using the New American Bible, add a chapter for any psalm after Psalm 9, which means that Psalm 103, as cited in Chapter 5, is Psalm 104 in the New American Bible.)

Timeline Work
Add the dates and events from 1243 through 1259 to your timeline.

Searching Scripture
Read the account of St. Paul's escape in a basket from Damascus in Acts 9:23-25. Compare and contrast this event to St. Thomas' escape.

Chapter 5—In Which Thomas Goes to Paris

REVIEW Vocabulary
on Sacred Scripture and *philosophy*   *Benediction*

in the *gesture* of a beggar   *Adoro Te*

??? Comprehension Questions/Narration Prompts
1. How old was Thomas when he was ordained a priest?
2. According to Thomas, where can one learn the most important things in the world? What is the finest book?
3. Why did Thomas feel he did not deserve to be called "wise"?

Forming Opinions/Drawing Conclusions
Thomas states that he and Albert walked from Cologne to Paris. Is it likely that someone would make this trip on foot today? In order to do so, how badly would you have to want to go? Describe some of the conditions Thomas might have encountered on this trip.

For Further Study
Two of Thomas' brothers were killed while helping the pope in his fight against the Roman emperor. The pope at this time was Gregory IX. The emperor, a Sicilian Norman, was Frederick II. Research the cause of this conflict, including the Council of Lyons.

Growing in Holiness
Although now considered one of the most learned men in Church history, Thomas did not feel worthy of a degree of Doctor of Theology. He viewed things with a heavenly perspective. Rather than comparing yourself to other people, compare yourself and your actions only to the perfection of God and the example He has set for us in Christ. How hard is this? What can you do to keep yourself on track?

✓ Checking the Catechism
Thomas tries to answer the question, "What is God?". Younger students should reference this topic in their own catechisms. Older students may read about God in text paragraphs 198-231 (36-43) in the *CCC*. If desired, complete Activity #38 in *100 Activities*.

Searching Scripture
Thomas uses Psalm 103 (104) as a topic for a theological speech. Read this psalm. What is its overall theme? What actions of God in this psalm help us answer Thomas' question, "What is God"?

Chapter 6—In Which Thomas Goes to Heaven

✖✖✖✖✖ Vocabulary

the *cobbled* streets of Bologna   *Corpus Christi*
was *dumbfounded*   *Summa Theologica*

??? Comprehension Questions/Narration Prompts

1. Why did Pope Urban IV order Thomas to write special prayers and hymns about the Blessed Sacrament?
2. What happened on December 6, 1273, that made Thomas long for death and made him feel that all his work was useless?
3. What were Thomas' dying words?

Forming Opinions/Drawing Conclusions

1. Pretend you are the brother who asked Thomas for help with the marketing. Speaking as this brother would speak (in the first person), tell what you thought about the friar who was assisting you as the incident was happening. Tell too how it felt when you found out that it was Thomas who had helped you.
2. Thomas' explanation of how to become a saint is simply, "Will it!" (page 66). What can you do differently to enact this philosophy?

For Further Study

Take the "Aquinas Challenge." Read through the following Thomas Aquinas quotations taken from text paragraphs of the *CCC*: 1718, 904, 43, 2763, 1308, 1902, and 155. (They are in this author's order of easiest to most difficult.) Paraphrase each quotation—that is, put it into your own words—and expand for a sentence or two on what this quotation implies. Continue through the list until you are stymied—use of a dictionary is encouraged. If you can make it through all seven quotations with complete understanding, perhaps you too can become a Doctor of the Church! If desired, continue with the challenge by reading more of his quotations as found in the "Index of Citations—Ecclesiastical Writers" in the back of the *CCC*. (Note that St. Thomas Aquinas is quoted sixty-one times in the *CCC*!)

✓ Checking the Catechism

Thomas demonstrates the virtue of obedience by assisting the lay brother when requested to do so. Older students may read text paragraphs 2247-2257 (178. 459, 464-465) in the *CCC*. If desired, complete Activity #58 in *100 Activities*.

Chapter 7—In Which Thomas Goes to Work

??? Comprehension Questions/Narration Prompts

1. What work does Thomas do as the Patron Saint of Catholic Schools?
2. What was the name of St. Thomas Aquinas' special society? When was it established? What was its purpose?

Forming Opinions/Drawing Conclusions

1. List at least three examples of humility that St. Thomas exhibited in his life. Give specific instances from events covered in Ms. Windeatt's biography.
2. Discuss why a children's religious club promoting purity is as important today as it was in St. Thomas' time. What can you do to guard your purity?

For Further Study

The thirteenth century has been called "the greatest century." Many of the barbarians were converted. Much of Europe was unified by the one true Faith. In this more settled time, there occurred an advancement of learning and a renewal of intellectual curiosity. Learned men not only continued to copy and preserve the teachings of the Church Fathers but also produced books of original thought. The writings of Greek philosophers came to Europe from the Muslims living in Spain. (Aristotle provided the rational foundation for the Christian philosophy of Thomas Aquinas.) Universities were established in order to educate monks beyond the level available in the monastery schools. The arts and sciences began to flourish as fields of study. Provide short descriptions for at least eight of the following thirteenth-century people and terms. If desired, summarize your research into a short report or oral presentation.)

St. Louis IX	Magna Charta
Pope Gregory IX	*chivalry*
Pope Innocent III	*scholasticism*
Dante	*mysticism*
Roger Bacon	Growth of universities—
Marco Polo	including the *Trivium*
St. Bonaventure	and *Quadtrivium*
Duns Scotus	*Gothic, Romanesque,* and
Chartres Cathedral	*Byzantine* architecture

Timeline Work

Add the dates and events from 1264 through 1340 to complete your timeline. Pay particular attention to the number of universities founded around this time period.

Patron Saints

The word "saint" comes from the Latin word *sanctus*, which translates as "consecrated" or "holy." Saints are men and women who have lived their lives (and very often gave them up freely) in such a way as to be rewarded with the Kingdom of God. The road to being officially recognized by the Church as a saint is a long one. In the earliest stage, the saint-in-the-making is identified as a "Servant of God." That stage is followed by the recognition of being "Venerable" and then "Blessed" before being recognized by the Church as a saint or "Friend of God." This official recognition by the Church as a saint comes at the conclusion of the process and ceremony called "canonization." These saints, who lived very holy lives, provide for us examples to follow so that we may, in turn, follow them to heaven. Based on the course of their lives and the circumstances surrounding them, some of the saints serve as "patrons" of certain peoples, places, things, and occupations, as they intercede for us before God. "Feast Days" are recognized for each saint. These feast days are very often the day of the year in which they died, especially if they gave up their lives for their faith. These special saints who gave up their lives for their faith are called "martyrs."

Patron Saints may be personal or general. A patron saint is personal for the Christian whose name he or she bears. Hence St. Gregory the Great is a patron saint for one whose name is Gregory. A patron saint may also be general for a group of people, e.g. St. Jerome is the Patron of Librarians while St. Anne is the Patroness of Canada. As such a saint may be a patron or a protector for those in particular professions or occupations, or may be invoked in times of special need.

"*. . . The Saint chosen acts in the role of sponsor for the person [people] in the courts of heaven . . . . our patron saint follows our earthly career with more than kindly interest. Do you know the life of your patron saint? You should, because he or she is your firm friend before the throne of God.*" – Richard Cardinal Cushing

By taking a Christian name, we not only honor the saints who have suffered and been glorified with Christ, but we also seek from the saints the example of their lives, fellowship in their communion, and aid by their intercession. A truly spiritual property is given to the Christian. His or her saint is not just a name, but also a pledge of a lifelong patron, a special intercessor or friend in heaven.

✎ Book Summary Test for *Saint Thomas Aquinas*

Directions: Answer in complete sentences. If necessary, use the back of the page for additional writing space. 100 possible points, 20 points for each answer.

1. What religious order did St. Thomas Aquinas' family want him to join? What religious order did he join? What happened when his family found out?

   _____

   _____

   _____

2. Name at least one hymn and one theological work that were written by St. Thomas.

   _____

   _____

   _____

3. During what century did St. Thomas live? List at least two other people named in this book who lived in this century.

   _____

   _____

4. Name at least two cities where St. Thomas lived. State why he moved to each place.

   _____

   _____

   _____

5. St. Thomas Aquinas has been called the "greatest theologian in the Church's history." He is also a Doctor of the Church—the "Angelic Doctor." What accomplishments helped St. Thomas to merit these titles?

   _____

   _____

   _____

   _____

   _____

Saint Thomas Aquinas, The Story of "The Dumb Ox"
Answer Key to Comprehension Questions

Introduction—In Which Thomas Tells Us of His Patronage
1. St. Thomas stated that the body is the least important part of a person. It is the soul that really matters.
2. Pope Leo XIII placed St. Thomas Aquinas as the Patron Saint of Catholic Schools in 1880.

Chapter 1—In Which Thomas Goes To School
1. Thomas was six years old when he was sent away to the boarding school at the abbey of Monte Cassino.
2. The abbey of Monte Cassino was a Benedictine abbey founded by St. Benedict. Their most important work was to praise God and to pray.

Chapter 2—In Which Thomas Goes to Naples
1. God gave Thomas the gifts of a quick mind and a good memory.
2. Thomas' two main attractions to the Dominican life were its preaching and teaching ministries, and the freedom of a friar on the move with no abbey to contain him.

Chapter 3—In Which Thomas Goes to Prison
1. Thomas went to the Dominican convent in Paris in an attempt to prevent his mother from stopping his vocation to the Dominican order.
2. Thomas' mother did not approve of his admission to the Dominican order as she did not approve of their begging, they had no famous abbey, and they preached to people of all classes and races. His family tried to get Thomas to give up his Dominican habit by locking him in the tower of their estate, feeding him a diet of bread and water, and tempting him with the companionship of a woman.
3. Thomas scared the girl out of the tower by attacking her with a burning log.

Chapter 4—In Which Thomas Goes to Cologne
1. God gave Thomas the great gift of purity in body and soul for the rest of his life as a reward for his perseverance in pursuing his religious vocation to the Dominicans.
2. With the assistance of his sisters, Thomas escaped from the tower through a narrow window in a basket. He had been a prisoner in the tower for eighteen months. Thomas spent much of his time reading and memorizing the Bible during his imprisonment in the tower.

Forming Opinions/Drawing Conclusions
Three possible reasons Thomas was called the "Dumb Ox of Sicily" include the following but other answers may also be logical:
1. He was born in the Kingdom of Sicily, which during Thomas' time, included not only the island of Sicily but also the southern third of what is now the country of Italy.
2. He was big and strong for his age.
3. He was not known to have a quick tongue.

Chapter 5—In Which Thomas Goes to Paris
1. Thomas was twenty-five years old when he was ordained a priest.
2. According to Thomas, the most important things in the world can be learned by looking at a crucifix, which he described as the "finest book."
3. Thomas felt he did not deserve to be called wise, as there were so many things he did not know and so many good acts he had left undone. Compared to the great mind of God, his mind was weak and human.

Chapter 6—In Which Thomas Goes To Heaven
1. Pope Urban IV ordered Thomas Aquinas to write special prayers and hymns about the Blessed Sacrament in preparation for his proclamation of the Feast of Corpus Christi (literally "the Body of Christ") as an official feast of the universal Church in 1264.
2. On that day, Thomas was granted a glimpse of heaven and the happiness of the blessed.
3. After receiving the Sacraments of Reconciliation and Holy Communion, Thomas recited the seven stanzas of *Adoro Te*, his composition in praise of Jesus in the Blessed Sacrament. (What prayers do you know that are worthy to be recited upon your deathbed?)

Chapter 7—In Which Thomas Goes to Work
1. Since being declared the Patron Saint of Catholic Schools, the work of Thomas Aquinas is to see that every Catholic child does well in school. He is a powerful intercessor.
2. The name of St. Thomas Aquinas' special society was *Angelic Warfare*. It was established in 1649 in Belgium. Its purpose was to help young people keep the purity of their bodies and souls spotless. (Note that this society is not currently active in the United States.)

Answer Key to Book Summary Test

1. St. Thomas Aquinas' family wanted him to join the Benedictine order and become the abbot of the monastery at Monte Cassino. Instead, Thomas joined the Dominican order at the age of eighteen. When his family found out, they came and forcibly took him back home. As he refused to leave the Dominican order, he was held captive in a tower in his family's castle for almost two years before his sisters freed him by lowering him from the tower in a basket.
2. Two familiar hymns written by St. Thomas Aquinas include *Adoro Te*, *Pange Lingua*, (The last two verses of this hymn are called the *Tantum Ergo* and are sung at Benediction; the beginning line in English is "Down in adoration falling"), and *O Salutaris* (*Verbum Supernum*). His two greatest written works are the *Summa Theologica* and *Summa Contra Gentiles*.
3. Thomas Aquinas lived in the thirteenth century, "the greatest century." Other historical figures named in this book include Sts. Dominic, Bonaventure, and Albert; Emperor Frederick I; and Popes Gregory IX, Innocent IV, and Urban IV. (Eight popes reigned during Thomas' lifetime.)
4. Thomas first went to Monte Cassino to attend school at the Benedictine monastery. Five years later, he moved to Naples to attend the university. He then went on several business trips to Paris, and then moved to Cologne to study under Fr. Albert. Then it was back to Paris where he received his bachelor's degree in theology, returning again to Cologne where he was ordained a priest and taught. He was then requested to go to Paris to study for his doctoral degree. He died on the road to Lyons, France.
5. St. Thomas, the "Dumb Ox", received a doctoral degree in theology. He wrote several works of theology including *Summa Contra Gentiles* and *Summa Theologica*, the latter of which is a five-volume book with over 3000 pages; it is still in print today—almost 750 years after its original publication date. He is probably the most quoted Catholic theologian. In the *CCC*, he is quoted sixty-one times with forty-eight of these quotations taken from his *Summa Theologica*. St. Thomas is called the "Angelic Doctor" due to the gift of purity that was given to him by God.

Study Guide for

The Patron Saint of First Communicants, The Story of Blessed Imelda Lambertini

Blessed Imelda Lambertini

When Blessed Imelda was born as a child
The whole town of Bologna nearly went wild.
Although not a boy,
Her birth brought great joy.
For free food and drink to the castle they filed.

Soon after her birth, her mom dreamed a great dream
In which her Imelda joined Dominic's team.
The child grew in grace
And fairness of face.
To receive Holy Communion was her one wish supreme.

She begged this from her parents, who could not comply
For this was a present that money can't buy.
Fourteen you must be—
A rule of the See—
She tried to be patient, on prayer did rely.

Agnes and Tarcisius, to them did she turn.
From their example wise things did she learn.
Church history she knew,
Saints' stories too,
To live all for Christ was her only concern.

When Imelda turned nine, to the convent she went.
Her parents were anxious but gave their consent.
Her job was the poor
To greet at the door.
Her vocation strong, despite youth, was content.

Yet her one desire was for Holy Communion
Where she and her Lord would achieve perfect union.
When He came to her heart,
He refused to depart;
He took her with Him to her all saints' reunion.

Think what you can learn from this saint and her tale.
How you can apply it to help you prevail.
Then mold what you do
And boldly pursue
Her pattern of holiness. Follow her trail.

Timeline of Events

Year	Event
1270	Marco Polo journeys to China; Phillip III becomes king of France
1274	Death of St. Thomas Aquinas
1291	End of crusades
1304	Birth of St. Bridget of Sweden; birth of Petrarch (Francesco Petrarca)
1307-21	Dante (Dante Alighieri born 1265) composes his Divine Comedy
1309-77	Papacy moved from Rome to Avignon, France, for reign of seven popes; beginning the "Babylonian Captivity"
1313	Birth of Giovanni Boccaccio, Florentine novelist (died 1375)
1321	Death of Dante
1322	Birth of Imelda Lambertini; pope forbids the use of counterpoint in church music
1323	St. Thomas Aquinas canonized
1324	Death of Marco Polo
1328	Birth of John Wycliffe in England; invention of the sawmill
1331	Imelda enters the convent at St. Mary Magdalen in Bologna, Italy
1332	Bubonic plague originates in India; first record of Parliament divided into two houses
1333	Death of Imelda Lambertini (declared "Blessed" in 1826)
1337-1453	Hundred Years' War between France and England
1341	Petrarch crowned poet in Rome
1345	Aztecs arrive in central Mexico
1347	Birth of St. Catherine of Siena
1347-53	Black Death (Bubonic Plague) sweeps Europe
1348-53	Boccaccio composes "Decameron"
1351	Petrarch composes his autobiography, *Epistle to Posterity*
1357	Birth of St. Vincent Ferrer
1361	Black Death reappears in England
1366	Petrarch composes "Canzoniere"
1368	Restoration of the Great Wall of China
1369	John Hus born (died in 1415)
1374	Death of Petrarch
1376	John Wycliffe calls for reform in the Church
1377	January 17th, Pope Gregory XI (died March 27, 1378) arrives in Rome to end the Church's "Babylonian Captivity"
1378-1417	Great Schism begins with election of both Pope Urban VI and Clement VII
1380	Death of St. Catherine of Siena; birth of St. Bernardine of Siena
1387-1400	Geoffrey Chaucer writes "Canterbury Tales"
1396	Birth of Johann Gutenberg, inventor of printing in Europe
1409	Council of Pisa called in attempt to end Great Schism
1412	Birth of St. Joan of Arc
1414	General Council of the Church at Constance, ending Great Schism and reforming the Church; Thomas á Kempis writes *Imitation of Christ*

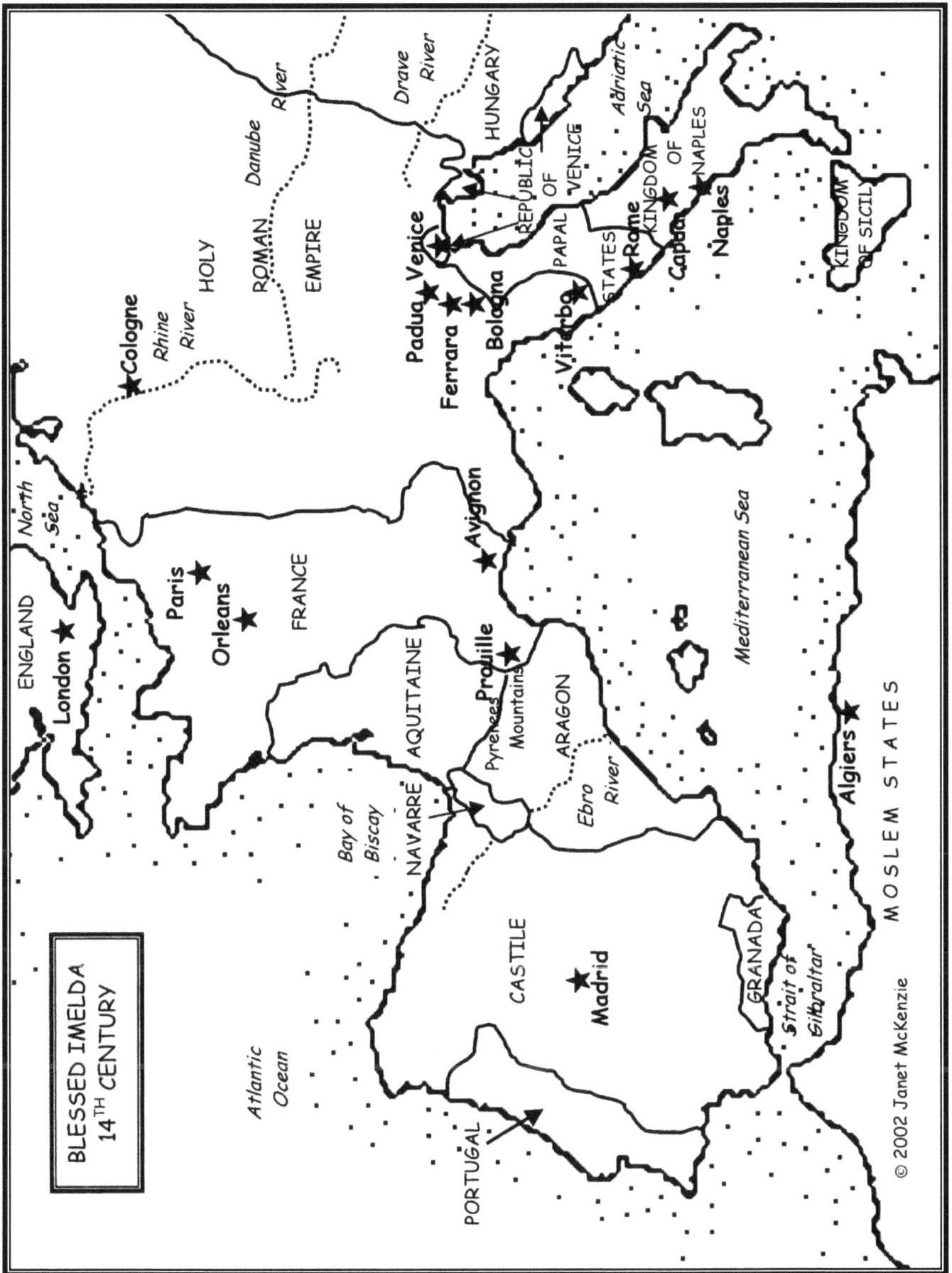

BLESSED IMELDA
14TH CENTURY

ENGLAND

London

North Sea

Atlantic Ocean

Bay of Biscay

FRANCE

Paris

Orleans

NAVARRE

AQUITAINE

Pyrenees Mountains

Prouille

ARAGON

Ebro River

CASTILE

Madrid

PORTUGAL

GRANADA

Strait of Gibraltar

Avignon

Mediterranean Sea

MOSLEM STATES

Algiers

Rhine River

HOLY

ROMAN

EMPIRE

Danube River

Drave River

HUNGARY

Cologne

Padua

Venice

Ferrara

Bologna

REPUBLIC OF VENICE

Adriatic Sea

Viterbo

PAPAL STATES

Rome

KINGDOM OF NAPLES

Capua

Naples

KINGDOM OF SICILY

© 2002 Janet McKenzie

Chapter 1–In Which Imelda Is Born

✖REVIEW✖ Vocabulary

deftly woven of colored reeds
in the *motley* procession were beggars

Peace of Christ
Baptism

??? Comprehension Questions/Narration Prompts

1. Where and when does this story take place?
2. What did Peter feel brought John, the baker's son, back home?
3. Why did Peter start out to see Donna Castora?
4. Why were the castle bells ringing?

Forming Opinions/Drawing Conclusions

1. Describe what a "face strongly marked with the peace of Christ" (page 3) looks like. What can you do to have the peace of Christ shine from your face?
2. "Sorrow, bravely borne, is nothing more than a key to the wonders of heaven" (page 5). Explain what this means.

For Further Study

The Angelus is a prayer of praise to the Blessed Virgin and a meditation on the mysteries of our Faith. Traditionally recited morning (in honor of the Resurrection), noon (in honor of the Passion), and evening (in honor of the Incarnation), its time was sounded by the ringing of the church bells that could be heard throughout the parish. Research the Angelus. Begin to pray it each day at noon. What is the proper way to ring the Angelus bells? Have a family member ring a bell this way each day at noon.

✝ Growing in Holiness

Peter and John talk about how many of us fail to thank God for His countless blessings. Spend extra time after receiving Holy Communion to thank God for the great gift of His Son. If possible, go each day—if only for several minutes—to thank Him before the Blessed Sacrament. IIe is truly present in every tabernacle of every Catholic Church. Be sure to acknowledge His Presence when you walk or drive by a Catholic Church—make the sign of the cross and say a short prayer such as "My Jesus, I believe that you are present in the most Blessed Sacrament."

✓ Checking the Catechism

". . . the saving waters of baptism" (page 10): Older students can read text paragraphs 1213-14, 1226-29, 1244-1246, 1256-59, 1263, and 1267 (34, 177, 200, 227, 252-263, 292, and 352) in the *Catechism of the Catholic Church (CCC)*. Younger students can complete Activity #10 in *100 Activities Based on the Catechism of the Catholic Church*.

Chapter 2–In Which Donna Castora Dreams of St. Dominic

⭐REVIEW⭐ Vocabulary

Listening to the sounds of *revelry*   *Franciscan*
to the *bedchamber*   *nun*

??? Comprehension Questions/Narration Prompts

1. How did the Lambertini's celebrate the birth of their daughter?
2. What was Donna Castora's dream and what did she feel it meant?
3. What did Donna Castora's brother, the archbishop, advise about the dream?

💡 Forming Opinions/Drawing Conclusions

The five forms of prayer are blessing and adoration, petition, intercession, thanksgiving, and praise. Find examples of each form of prayer within the first two chapters of this book. State how each form can be used by you in prayer each day.

📖 For Further Study

Research the life of St. Dominic, who died in 1221. Prepare an oral presentation, or write a brief report on St. Dominic. Include the order he founded, the stated purpose of the order, the convent of nuns he established in 1206, and his holy death. What helped him become a saint?

✝ Growing in Holiness

"Every child born into the world is given the grace to become a saint. Castora, you must teach little Imelda this truth and help her to use the graces God gives her" (page 21). Pray daily for more graces to persevere in the spiritual life. Be aware each moment of the graces and opportunities for grace that God offers you. Receive Holy Communion as often as possible.

📅 Timeline Work

Taping sheets of plain paper end-to-end, make a timeline representing the years from 1270 through 1414. Let three inches equal 25 years. Mark on your timeline the dates and events from 1270 through 1328, using information from page 20.

📖 Searching Scripture

Read some dreams as recorded in Holy Scripture: Genesis 37:5-11, Matthew 1:18-24 and Matthew 2:12. Where are other dreams recorded in Scripture?

Chapter 3–In Which Imelda Longs for Our Lord

✖REVIEW✖ Vocabulary

Imelda *caressed* the beads gently   *Blessed Trinity*
the child's face grew *wistful*   *Tabernacle*

⁇⁇ Comprehension Questions/Narration Prompts

1. What were some of the gifts that God had bestowed upon Imelda?
2. What did Imelda want as a present for her fifth birthday? Why was she not to get it?
3. What was Imelda's favorite gift of all the presents received?

For Further Study

Read the story of Tarcisius found on pages 35-37 below. Try to find additional information about St. Tarcisius in other sources. Write a summary of his life.

✝ Growing in Holiness

Imelda was the daughter of very wealthy parents. Notice her plush surroundings and lavish gifts (pages 26 and 27). Yet her favorite birthday gift was a rosary given to her by her mother. With all the extravagance around her, she still put much importance in Godly things. Re-evaluate your priorities. What are your feelings about presents? What value do you place on religious or spiritual gifts? Where do you spend your money and your time? Are you trying to accumulate worldly possessions or heavenly treasures? What adjustments do you need to make in your life so as to more closely imitate Imelda?

Geography

Trace the map on page 21. Color these seas blue: Atlantic, North, Adriatic, and Mediterranean as well as these rivers: Rhine, Danube, Ebro, and Drave. Locate Crete, mentioned on page 12, on a modern map. (The remainder of the map will be completed in Chapter 4.)

✓ Checking the Catechism

Complete Activity #52 in *100 Activities* on the Holy Eucharist. Older students may read text paragraphs 1322-44 (271-276) in the *CCC* on the topic of the Holy Eucharist.

Searching Scripture

"When we help the poor and sick, we're really helping Him!" (page 24). Read Matthew 25:31-46.

Chapter 4–In Which Imelda Shares Her Knowledge of the Dominican Order

---

✂REVIEW✂ Vocabulary

to those *pioneer* days in Bologna   *Blessed Sacrament*
the Latin *inscription*   *Divine Praises*

??? Comprehension Questions/Narration Prompts

1. Who were Imelda's imaginary companions?
2. What was Imelda's attitude toward the required wait for Holy Communion?
3. Why was Beatrice uneasy over Imelda's account of the Dominican saints?
4. What was Imelda's daily prayer for her friend, Peter, the basket-maker?
5. List the two wishes Imelda expressed while visiting the Convent of St. Agnes.

💡 Forming Opinions/Drawing Conclusions

Foreshadowing is a writer's technique, in which hints are given about what is going to happen in the story. As she waited to receive God in Holy Communion, Imelda stated, "He has a reason for making me wait. . . . Someday I'll understand what it is" (page 37). What may this statement be foreshadowing? (If you are not familiar with the life of Blessed Imelda, list several options stating why God is making her wait.)

📖 For Further Study

Research the life of St. Agnes, who died during the Christian persecutions under the emperor Diocletian in the fourth century. Cardinal Wiseman's book, *Fabiola*, contains much about her life. Summarize your research into a report.

✝ Growing in Holiness

Imelda had great trust in God's care for her: "The best thing to do was to bear the disappointment bravely and trust that He would let everything turn to good" (page 37). Think about the last disappointment you had. What was your attitude? What do you think you could do differently next time in order to mimic more closely the attitude of Imelda? How disappointed are you when you are unable to receive the Lord in Holy Communion?

🗺 Geography

Complete the map started in Chapter 3 by labeling the cities red and the countries green. On the map provided, cities are indicated with a star, and countries are in capital letters. Using a modern map, locate the countries in which these cities are located today.

Chapter 5—In Which Imelda Joins the Convent of St. Mary Magdalen

Vocabulary
asked the Prioress *shrewdly*
might be a little *timid*

scapular
choir

Comprehension Questions/Narration Prompts
1. What convent did Imelda enter as a religious? How old was she?
2. As she gave herself to God and received the habit, for what did she ask?
3. List some of the virtues Imelda was expected to acquire as a novice.
4. What was Imelda's new duty in the convent?

Forming Opinions/Drawing Conclusions
List some of the ways in which Imelda failed as a novice. Describe the procedure of the convent in dealing with these faults. If this procedure were enacted in your house, how would you and other family members react?

For Further Study
There are several references to St. Benedict in this chapter. Research the life of St. Benedict, the Rule of St. Benedict, and his original monastery—Monte Cassino, which was called the "School of the Lord's Service."

Growing in Holiness
"'Peter, I do pray for you,' she said gently. 'Every day. You know that. But I fear I can never pray for you or anyone as I really wish'" (page 58). And "When will they let me pray for people as I really want to pray?" (page 58) Imelda is crying out to receive Holy Communion so that she may pray for people in a better way—with the Lord in her heart. Remember each time you receive the Eucharist to ask that the graces obtained with your reception be applied to specific intentions. This can be done for each act you do—each prayer you make—but the graces of the Eucharist are infinite, whereas the graces we can obtain for the recitation of the rosary, for example, are limited. With each Holy Communion, remember each loved one, each "cause" (peace in our world, an end to abortion, etc.), your own spiritual needs, the intentions of the Holy Father, and those for whom you have promised to pray. Ask your guardian angel to help you remember those you have promised to pray for—or have your angel offer those intentions in prayer for you.

Timeline Work
Add the dates and events from 1331 through 1361 to your timeline.

Chapter 6–In Which Our Lord Comes to Imelda in an Unexpected Way

---

✴REVIEW✴ Vocabulary
these men would *rival* the great Dante   *confessor*
obscured by the heavy iron grating   *Consecration*

??? Comprehension Questions/Narration Prompts
1. What was preventing Imelda from receiving Communion at the age of eleven?
2. What did Imelda state as requirements for receiving Holy Communion?
3. What reason did the nuns give for Imelda's tears after Mass on the vigil of the Feast of Ascension? What was the real reason for her tears?
4. What is "The Miracle" of this chapter?

For Further Study
Research the Italian writers Petrarch and Boccaccio. What were their full names? When and where did they live? What type of writing did they do? What were the major literary contributions of each? Compare them to Dante, the great Italian poet who lived from 1265-1321. Write a brief report on these three men.

✝ Growing in Holiness
Our Lord came to Imelda in a miraculous way. Remember that each time He comes to us in Holy Communion, it too is a miracle. Jesus, the second Person of the Blessed Trinity, becomes physically present in each of us. As the Trinity is three Persons in one God, we also receive God the Father and God the Holy Spirit in each Communion. If we all truly knew and understood this in our minds and hearts, would we ever get off our knees after Holy Communion?

✓ Checking the Catechism
1. To preach and to teach is the mission of the Dominican order. The mission of the Church is to "teach, sanctify, and rule the faithful in the name of Christ." Complete Activities #77 and #78 in *100 Activities*. Read corresponding text paragraphs in the *CCC*: 77, 751-53, 770, 777-80, and 866-70 (144, 150, 173, 175, 193, and 201).
2. Imelda lists several parts of the Mass in anticipation of the time for Holy Communion. Study the Holy Mass. Younger students can complete Activity #12 in *100 Activities* while older students read text paragraphs 1345-55 and 1382-89 (277 and 287-289) in the *CCC*.

📖 Searching Scripture
Read Matthew 19:13-15.

Chapter 7–In Which Imelda's Dream Comes True

⭑REVIEW⭑ Vocabulary

All *clamored* for the truth   *Holy Thursday*
did not *deter* him   *Last Supper*

??? Comprehension Questions/Narration Prompts
1. How long did the nuns remain in thanksgiving after the miracle of the Host?
2. After seeing Imelda, how did the Prioress describe Holy Communion?
3. What was the reaction of Imelda's parents when they learned of her death?
4. What was the first miracle attributed to Imelda's intercession after her death?

Forming Opinions/Drawing Conclusions
1. As the nuns gazed upon Imelda after she received her first Communion, they recalled her words: "How can anyone receive our Lord and not die of happiness?" (page 76). What writing technique does Ms. Windeatt use with this expression?
2. In your opinion, which miracle—the miracle of Imelda's first Holy Communion or the miracle of Peter's restored sight—was the greater miracle? Support your argument with quotations from the book, Scripture, or Catholic doctrine.

For Further Study
Read the two papal encyclicals included on pages 39-42: *Quam Singulari*, Decree on First Communion; and *Sacra Tridentina*, On Frequent and Daily Reception of Holy Communion. (Note that both documents have been abbreviated for use with this study guide.)

✝ Growing in Holiness
Be sure to mediate on Jesus' great love for you after receiving Him in the Eucharist. As the structure of the Mass does not allow an adequate thanksgiving to be made before Mass is completed, remain in thanksgiving after Mass for several minutes. Remember that the nuns remained in humble thanksgiving for over an hour.

Timeline Work
Add the dates and events from 1366 through 1414 to complete your timeline.

Searching Scripture
". . . when he makes the Heavenly Father a present. The smallest gift comes back a hundredfold. I gave my child to God, and now He has given her back to me—a *saint*!" (page 81) Read Matthew 19:27-29 and 2 Corinthians 9:6-8.

More Saints of the Eucharist

Research the lives of the following saints who are known to have had a special devotion to the Holy Eucharist:

1. St. Tarcisius
2. St. Agnes
3. St. Pius X
4. St. Paschal Baylon
5. St. Gerard
6. St. Gemma
7. St. Peter Julian Eymard
8. St. Cyril of Jerusalem
9. St. Thomas Aquinas
10. St. Therese of the Child Jesus
11. St. Teresa of Avila
12. St. Alphonsus Liguori
13. St. Margaret Mary
14. St. Isidore the Farmer
15. Blessed Peter Vigne
16. St. Pio of Pietrelcina

Prayer of St. Pio of Pietrelcina after Holy Communion

Stay with me, Lord, for it is necessary to have You present so that I do not forget You. You know how easily I abandon You.

Stay with me, Lord, because I am weak and I need Your strength that I may not fall so often.

Stay with me, Lord, for You are my life, and without You, I am without fervor.

Stay with me, Lord, You are my light, and without You, I am in darkness.

Stay with me, Lord, to show me Your will.

Stay with me, Lord, so that I hear Your voice and follow You.

Stay with me, Lord, for I desire to love You very much, and always be in Your company.

Stay with me, Lord, if You wish me to be faithful to You.

Stay with me, Lord, for as poor as my soul is, I wish it to be a place of consolation for You, a nest of Love.

Stay with me, Jesus, for it is getting late and the day is coming to a close and life passes, death, judgment, eternity approaches. It is necessary to renew my strength, so that I will not stop along the way and for that, I need You. It is getting late and death approaches. I fear the darkness, the temptations, the dryness, the cross, the sorrows. Oh, how I need You, dear Jesus, in this night of exile!

Stay with me tonight, Jesus, in life with all its dangers, I need you. Let me recognize You as Your disciples did at the breaking of the bread, so that the Eucharistic Communion be the light which disperses the darkness, the force with sustains me, the unique joy of my heart.

Stay with me, Lord, because at the hour of my death, I want to remain united to You, if not by Communion, at least by grace and love.

Stay with me, Jesus. I do not ask for divine consolation, because I do not merit it, but, the gift of Your Presence, oh yes, I ask this of You!

Stay with me, Lord, for it is You alone I look for, Your love, Your grace, Your will, Your heart, Your spirit, because I love You and ask no other reward but to love You more and more.

With a firm love, I will love You with all my heart while on earth and continue to love You perfectly during all eternity. Amen.

✎ Book Summary Test for *Patron Saint of First Communicants*

Directions: Answer in complete sentences. If necessary, use the back of the page for additional writing space. 100 possible points, 20 points for each answer.

1. What was Imelda's dream—her burning desire—from the age of five?

   _____

   _____

2. Describe Imelda Lambertini's family and her home life.

   _____

   _____

   _____

3. At what age did Imelda enter the Dominican convent of St. Mary Magdalen? What was her job there?

   _____

   _____

   _____

4. How old was Imelda when she died? In what year did she die? Describe the cause of her death.

   _____

   _____

   _____

5. How did Imelda's family life contribute to the formation of her religious life? What is the importance of establishing holy families where the Faith is taught, nurtured, and lived? What can you do to make your family more like the Holy Family of Nazareth?

   _____

   _____

   _____

The Patron Saint of First Communicants, The Story of Blessed Imelda Lambertini
Answer Key to Comprehension Questions

Chapter 1—In Which Imelda Is Born
1. The story of Blessed Imelda takes place in Bologna, a city in northern Italy, beginning in the year of her birth, 1322.
2. Peter feels that John's son returned home "only because of prayer" (page 2).
3. Peter starts out to see Donna Castora to thank her for her prayers for Phillip and tell her that Phillip has come back. However, he does not get to tell her due to the excitement of the birth of Donna's child.
4. The castle bells were ringing to celebrate the birth of the Lambertini's daughter. Peter states that according to common custom, the bells were usually only rung if the new child was a boy.

Chapter 2—In Which Donna Castora Dreams of St. Dominic
1. The Lambertini's celebrated the birth of their daughter by providing free food and wine to all.
2. Donna Castora dreamed that she had met St. Dominic and that he had given her a special smile and blessing. She felt that great things were in store for Imelda.
3. Donna Castora's brother, the archbishop, advised her that some dreams are sent for a special purpose, but that she must not read too much into the dream.

Chapter 3—In Which Imelda Longs for Our Lord
1. Some of the gifts that God had bestowed upon Imelda included physical beauty, a quick mind, and an unselfish spirit. She loved to make others happy.
2. For her fifth birthday, Imelda wished to receive our Lord in Holy Communion "just like grown-up people do" (page 30). Her parents were unable to grant this wish as Church regulations at that time required that a child be fourteen years old to receive Holy Communion. (This rule was changed to the age seven by Pope Pius X in 1910.)
3. Of all her gifts, Imelda's favorite was the pearl rosary given to Imelda by her mother.

Chapter 4—In Which Imelda Shares Her Knowledge of the Dominican Order
1. Tarcisius and St. Agnes were Imelda's imaginary companions. She often asked them to help her love God as He wishes to be loved.
2. By the time she was nine, Imelda's attitude toward receiving Holy Communion was one of patient resignation. She felt God had a reason for making her wait to receive Him, and she tried to be satisfied in waiting as He wished.
3. Beatrice was uneasy over Imelda's account of the Dominican saints as she felt such deep thoughts were far beyond Imelda's years.
4. Imelda prayed daily that God would give Peter back his sight.
5. During her visit to the Sisters of St. Agnes Convent, Imelda wished that she had known Blessed Diana and that she could love our Lord as the sisters did.

Chapter 5—In Which Imelda Joins the Convent of St. Mary Magdalen
1. Imelda entered the Dominican convent of St. Mary Magdalen in Bologna, Italy, at age nine.
2. As she gave herself to God's service and received the Dominican habit, Imelda asked for "God's mercy and yours" [the superior's] (page 54).
3. Some of the virtues Imelda was expected to acquire as a novice included obedience and humility. She needed to be willing to act as a servant to others and to bear all trials.
4. In the convent Imelda was assigned charge of the poor who came to the monastery for food.

Chapter 6—In Which Our Lord Comes to Imelda in an Unexpected Way

1. The tradition of the Church (Church rule) during the fourteenth century was that children must be fourteen years of age to receive Holy Communion.
2. Imelda stated that neither the angels nor saints in heaven can receive Holy Communion; but anyone who has the True Faith and keeps the Commandments (is in the state of grace) may receive our Lord in the Eucharist.
3. Several of the nuns believed that Imelda was crying as the spring weather was causing her to be homesick. The real reason for her tears, however, was that she was disappointed about the continued delay in receiving our Lord in Holy Communion.
4. The miracle of this chapter is the presence of a consecrated Host floating above Imelda's head. This Host, accompanied by a strange light and a marvelous fragrance of flowers, had moved from above the altar, through the cloister grating, and across the chapel to rest above Imelda.

Chapter 7—In Which Imelda's Dream Comes True

1. The nuns remained in humble thanksgiving for more than an hour after witnessing the miracle of the floating Host.
2. After leaving Imelda in the chapel, the Prioress described Holy Communion as the greatest privilege in the world—a proof, if one were needed, of God's immense love for all mankind.
3. Thanks to the intercession of Imelda, her parents came to the convent after her death, dry-eyed and calm. While grieving, they accepted God's will with eagerness and trust, without question or complaint.
4. The first miracle attributed to the intercession of Imelda after her death was the return of vision to the blind basket-maker, Peter.

Answer Key to Book Summary Test

1. From the age of five, Imelda was filled with a burning desire to receive our Lord in Holy Communion. (The Church regulations at the time required that a child be at least fourteen years of age before they were able to receive the Sacrament of the Eucharist.)
2. Imelda Lambertini's family was wealthy; her father, a lawyer and nobleman, was powerful in the government and well respected. Both of Imelda's parents were pious Catholics. Imelda had one uncle who was an Augustinian priest, another uncle who was the archbishop of Crete, and an aunt who was a convent abbess. Imelda lived in a lavishly decorated castle, surrounded by luxury. She left her home at the age of nine to live the life of a humble nun in a Dominican convent.
3. Imelda entered the Dominican convent of St. Mary Magdalen just outside the city of Bologna, Italy, at the age of nine. In the convent Imelda was assigned charge of the poor who came to the monastery for food.
4. Imelda died in 1333 at the age of eleven. She died of joy after finally receiving our Lord in the Holy Eucharist on the vigil of the Feast of the Ascension after our Lord miraculously indicated that He desired that she receive Him.
5. Answers will vary.

The Story of Tarcisius[1]

(Note: This story takes place early in the fourth century in Rome under the rule of Maximian Herculeus, brother of Diocletian. The scene regarding Tarcisius occurs on the day before a group of Christian prisoners are to be brought into the Coliseum to "fight" with the wild beasts. On these days the Roman guards allowed the prisoners to be visited by their family and friends. They enjoyed a free supper—a luxurious public feast. It was arranged to have sufficient amounts of the Bread of Life smuggled into the prisoners to allow them to partake of this Bread on the morning of their battle. However, many of the adult ministers of the Eucharist had been identified and could not safely travel by day unless thoroughly disguised.)

The Sacred Bread was prepared, and the priest turned around from the altar on which It was placed, to see who would be Its safest bearer. Before any other could step forward, the young acolyte Tarcisius knelt at his feet.

"You are too young, my child," said the kind priest, filled with admiration of the picture before him.

"My youth, holy Father, will be my best protection. Oh! Do not refuse me this great honor." Tears sparkled in the boy's eyes, and his cheeks glowed with emotion, as he spoke these words. He stretched forth his hands eagerly, and his entreaty was so full of fervor and courage, that the plea was irresistible. The priest took the Divine Mysteries, wrapped Them up carefully in a linen cloth, then in an outer covering, and put Them on Tarcisius' palms.

"Remember, Tarcisius, what a Treasure is entrusted to your feeble care," he said. "Avoid public places as you go along. Remember that holy things must not be delivered to dogs, nor pearls be cast before swine. You will keep safe God's Sacred Gifts?"

"I will die rather than betray Them," answered the holy youth, as he folded the heavenly trust into the bosom of his tunic. With cheerful reverence he set out on his errand.

As he was approaching the door of a large mansion, its mistress, a rich lady without children, saw him coming. She was struck with his beauty and sweetness, as, with arms folded on his breast, he hastened on.

"Stop one moment, dear child," she said, putting herself in his way. "Tell me your name. Where do your parents live?"

"I am Tarcisius, an orphan boy," he replied, looking up smilingly. "I have no home, except one which it might displease you to hear."

"Then come into my house and rest. I wish to speak to you. Oh, if only I had a boy like you!"

"Not now, noble lady, not now. I have entrusted to me a most solemn and sacred duty, and I must not tarry a moment in its performance."

"Then promise to come to me tomorrow. This is my house."

---

[1]His Eminence Cardinal Wiseman, (Modern English Edition by the Daughters of St. Paul) *Fabiola or the Church of the Catacombs* (Derby, New York: St. Paul Publications, 1955), pages 384-389.

"If I am alive, I will," answered the boy, with an inspired look, which made him seem to her to be a messenger from a higher sphere. She watched him for a long time, and after some deliberation resolved to follow him. Soon, however, she heard a tumult of horrid shouts, which made her pause on her way. When they had ceased, she went on again.

In the meantime, Tarcisius, with his thoughts fixed on better things than her inheritance, hurried on, and shortly came into an open space, where boys, just out from school, were beginning to play.

"We need one more to make up the game. Where shall we get him?" asked their leader.

"How wonderful!" exclaimed another. "Here comes Tarcisius, whom I haven't seen for ages. He used to be excellent at all kinds of games. Come, Tarcisius," he added, seizing him by the arms, "where are you going? Come and play with us like a good fellow."

"I can't, Petilus. Not right now. I really can't. I'm going on business of great importance."

"But you shall," exclaimed the first speaker, a strong bully, laying hold of him. "I will have no sulking when I want anything done. So come and play with us at once."

"I beg of you," said Tarcisius, "please let me go."

"Certainly not," replied the other. "What is that which you are carrying in your bosom? A letter, I suppose. Well, it will not rot by being out of its nest for half an hour. Give it to me. I will put it in a safe place while we play." And he snatched at the Sacred Deposit.

"Never, never," answered Tarcisius, looking up toward heaven.

"I will see it," insisted the other. "I want to know what this wonderful secret is." And he began pulling Tarcisius about roughly.

A crowd of men from the neighborhood soon gathered. They asked eagerly what the matter was.

"What is it? What can it be?" they asked one another. At that moment Fulvius chanced to pass by. He joined the circle around the combatants. He immediately recognized Tarcisius, whom he had seen at the Ordination[2]. Being asked, as a better-dressed man, the same question, he replied contemptuously, as he turned on his heel, "What is it? Why, only a Christian ass[3], bearing the Mysteries."

A general demand was made to Tarcisius to yield up his charge.

"Never while there is life in me," was his only reply.

A heavy blow from a smith's fist half stunned him. Blood flowed from the wound. Another and another blow followed, until covered with bruises, but his arms still crossed tightly upon his breast, Tarcisius fell heavily on the ground. The mob closed in upon him, and were just about to seize him to tear open his thrice-holy trust, when they felt themselves pushed aside right and left by some giant force. Some went reeling to the further side of the square, others were spun around and around, they knew not how,

---

[2]Each December the popes of this time held an ordination ceremony to create priests, deacons, and bishops for different places. This refers to the ordination ceremony that had occurred the past December by Pope Marcellinus.
[3]It was a common belief of pagans at this time that Christians worshipped the head of an ass.

until they fell where they were. The rest retired hastily before the tall athletic officer, who had scattered the others. He had no sooner cleared the ground than he fell on his knees, and, with tears in his eyes, raised up the bruised and dying boy as tenderly as a mother would have done. In the gentlest of tones he asked him, "Are you badly hurt, Tarcisius?"

"Never mind me, Quadratus[4]," he answered, opening his eyes and smiling, "I am carrying the Divine Mysteries. Take care of Them."

The soldier raised the boy in his arms with tenfold reverence, aware that he was bearing, not only the sweet victim of a youthful sacrifice, a martyr's relics, but also the very King and Lord of Martyrs, the divine Victim of eternal salvation. The child's head leaned in confidence on the strong soldier's neck, but his arms and hands never left their watchful custody of the confided Gift. His gallant bearer felt no weight in the hallowed double burden which he carried. No one stopped him, until a lady met him and stared amazedly at him. She drew nearer, and looked closer at what he carried.

"Is it possible?" she exclaimed with terror. "Is this Tarcisius, whom I met a few moments ago, so fair and lovely? Who did this?"

"Madam," replied Quadratus, "they have murdered him because he was a Christian."

The lady looked for an instant on the child's countenance. He opened his eyes, looked at her, smiled, and expired. From that look came the light of faith—she hastened to be a Christian too.

The venerable Dionysius[5] could hardly see for weeping, as he removed the child's hands, and took from his bosom, unviolated, the Holy of Holies. He thought Tarcisius looked more like an Angel now, sleeping the Martyr's slumber, than he did when living scarcely an hour before.

Quadratus carried him to the cemetery of Callistus where he was buried.

———————————————

Damasus, who was pope from 366-384, composed poems in honor of martyrs and popes, and had them inscribed on marble slabs in front of their tombs. The poem, or epigram, by Pope St. Damasus that commemorates St. Tarcisius reminds us of his martyrdom:

"When a wicked group of fanatics flung themselves
on Tarcisius who was carrying the Eucharist,
wanting to profane the Sacrament, the boy preferred
to give up his life rather than yield up
the Body of Christ to those rabid dogs."
(Excerpted from http://brogilbert.org/body_christ/5body_belief.htm)

———————————————

[4] Quadratus was a Roman officer and a Christian.
[5] Dionysius was a pious priest who lived with the family of Saint Agnes.

Sacra Tridentina
(On Frequent and Daily Reception of Holy Communion)

Issued and approved by Pope Pius X on December 20, 1905

. . . Accordingly, the Sacred Congregation of the Council, in a Plenary Session held on December 16, 1905, submitted this matter to a very careful study, and after sedulously examining the reasons adduced on either side, determined and declared as follows:

1. Frequent and daily Communion, as a practice most earnestly desired by Christ our Lord and by the Catholic Church, should be open to all the faithful, of whatever rank and condition of life; so that no one who is in the state of grace, and who approaches the Holy Table with a right and devout intention (*recta piaque mente*) can be prohibited therefrom.

2. A right intention consists in this: that he who approaches the Holy Table should do so, not out of routine, or vain glory, or human respect, but that he wish to please God, to be more closely united with Him by charity, and to have recourse to this divine remedy for his weakness and defects.

3. Although it is especially fitting that those who receive Communion frequently or daily should be free from venial sins, at least from such as are fully deliberate, and from any affection thereto, nevertheless, it is sufficient that they be free from mortal sin, with the purpose of never sinning in the future; and if they have this sincere purpose, it is impossible by that daily communicants should gradually free themselves even from venial sins, and from all affection thereto.

4. Since, however, the Sacraments of the New Law, though they produce their effect *ex opere operato*, nevertheless, produce a great effect in proportion as the dispositions of the recipient are better, therefore, one should take care that Holy Communion be preceded by careful preparation, and followed by an appropriate thanksgiving, according to each one's strength, circumstances and duties.

5. That the practice of frequent and daily Communion may be carried out with greater prudence and more fruitful merit, the confessor's advice should be asked. Confessors, however, must take care not to dissuade anyone from frequent or daily Communion, provided he is found to be in a state of grace and approaches with a right intention.

6. But since it is plain that by the frequent or daily reception of the Holy Eucharist union with Christ is strengthened, the spiritual life more abundantly sustained, the soul more richly endowed with virtues, and the pledge of everlasting happiness more securely bestowed on the recipient, therefore, parish priests, confessors and preachers, according to the approved teaching of the *Roman Catechism* should exhort the faithful frequently and with great zeal to this devout and salutary practice.

7. Frequent and daily Communion is to be promoted especially in religious Institutes of all kinds; with regard to which, however, the Decree *Quemadmodum* issued on December 17, 1890, by the Sacred Congregation of Bishops and Regulars, is to remain in force. It is to be promoted especially in ecclesiastical seminaries, where students are preparing for the service of the altar; as also in all Christian establishments which in any way provide for the care of the young (*ephebeis*).

8. In the case of religious Institutes, whether of solemn or simple vows, in whose rules, or constitutions, or calendars, Communion is assigned to certain fixed days, such regulations are to be considered as directive and not preceptive. The prescribed number of Communions should be regarded as a minimum but not a limit to the devotion of the religious. Therefore, access to the Eucharistic Table, whether it be rather frequently or daily, must always be freely open to them according to the norms above laid down in this Decree. Furthermore, in order that all religious of both sexes may clearly understand the prescriptions of this Decree, the Superior of each house will provide that it be read in community, in the vernacular, every year within the octave of the Feast of Corpus Christi.

9. Finally, after the publication of this Decree, all ecclesiastical writers are to cease from contentious controversy concerning the dispositions requisite for frequent and daily Communion.

All this having been reported to His Holiness, Pope Pius X, by the undersigned Secretary of the Sacred Congregation in an audience held on December 17, 1905, His Holiness ratified this Decree, confirmed it and ordered its publication, anything to the contrary notwithstanding. He further ordered that it should be sent to all local Ordinaries and regular prelates, to be communicated by them to their respective seminaries, parishes, religious institutes, and priests; and that in their report on the state of their dioceses or institutes they should inform the Holy See concerning the execution of the prescriptions therein enacted.

Given at Rome, the 20th day of December, 1905
Vincent, Card. Bishop of Palestrina, Prefect
Cajetan DeLai, Secretary
(Excerpted and edited from the Eternal Word Television Network online library at www.ewtn.com/library/CURIA/CDWFREQ.HTM)

Quam Singulari (Decree on First Communion)

Sacred Congregation of the Discipline of the Sacraments—August 8, 1910

. . . this Sacred Congregation of the Discipline of the Sacraments, in a general meeting held on July 15, 1910, in order to . . . bring about that children even from their tender years may be united to Jesus Christ, may live His life, and obtain protection from all danger of corruption, has deemed it needful to prescribe the following rules which are to be observed everywhere for the First Communion of children.

1. The age of discretion, both for Confession and for Holy Communion, is the time when a child begins to reason, that is about the seventh year, more or less. From that time on begins the obligation of fulfilling the precept of both Confession and Communion.

2. A full and perfect knowledge of Christian doctrine is not necessary either for First Confession or for First Communion. Afterwards, however, the child will be obliged to learn gradually the entire Catechism according to his ability.

3. The knowledge of religion which is required in a child in order to be properly prepared to receive First Communion is such that he will understand according to his capacity those Mysteries of faith which are necessary as a means of salvation (*necessitate medii*) and that he can distinguish between the Bread of the Eucharist and ordinary, material bread, and thus he may receive Holy Communion with a devotion becoming his years.

4. The obligation of the precept of Confession and Communion which binds the child particularly affects those who have him in charge, namely, parents, confessor, teachers and the pastor. It belongs to the father, or the person taking his place, and to the confessor, according to the Roman Catechism, to admit a child to his First Communion.

5. The pastor should announce and hold a General Communion of the children once a year or more often, and he should on these occasions admit not only the First Communicants but also others who have already approached the Holy Table with the above-mentioned consent of their parents or confessor. Some days of instruction and preparation should be previously given to both classes of children.

6. Those who have charge of the children should zealously see to it that after their First Communion these children frequently approach the Holy Table, even daily if possible, as Jesus Christ and Mother Church desire, and let this be done with a devotion becoming their age. They must also bear in mind that very grave duty which obliged them to have the children attend the public Catechism classes; if this is not done, then they must supply religious instruction in some other way.

7. The custom of not admitting children to Confession or of not giving them absolution when they have already attained the use of reason must be entirely abandoned. The Ordinary shall see to it that this condition ceases absolutely, and he may, if necessary, use legal measures accordingly.

8. The practice of not administering the Viaticum and Extreme Unction to children who have attained the use of reason, and of burying them with the rite used for infants is a most intolerable abuse. The Ordinary should take very severe measures against those who do not give up the practice.

His Holiness, Pope Pius X, in an audience granted on the seventh day of this month, approved all the above decisions of this Sacred Congregation, and ordered this Decree to be published and promulgated.

He furthermore commanded that all the Ordinaries make this Decree known not only to the pastors and the clergy, but also to the people, and he wishes that it be read in the vernacular every year at the Easter time. The Ordinaries shall give an account of the observance of this Decree together with other diocesan matters every five years.

(The above document was taken from the Eternal Word Television Network web site at www.ewtn.com/library/CURIA/CDWFIRST.HTM and has been abridged.)

Study Guide for

Saint Catherine of Siena, The Story of the Girl Who Saw Saints in the Sky

St. Catherine of Siena

In Siena, Italy, as a young girl,
She saw saints in the sky like pictures unfurl.
She tried to flee,
A hermit to be,
She offered up much—even cut off her curl.

Catherine lived like a maid in her own family's house.
No husband for her—God was her loved spouse.
More saints did she see.
She wanted to be
Not a nun, but live in the world, in her house.

She prayed hard for sinners, lived in a small room,
Caught smallpox, and 'fore the disease did consume,
To Dominic she went—
Her mom gave her consent—
She joined the order, a habit to assume.

God gave her His ring as her worthy reward
For honoring Him as her God and her Lord—
Lived in the world still,
The Lord's Will to fulfill,
Moved back with her fam'ly, her maid's life restored.

She took care of lepers and young men in jail.
She bathed them and fed them, God's Will helped prevail.
For others pain bore,
To her was no chore.
For sinners she suffered each day without fail.

In the summer into France to the pope she did go.
His Avignon residence was wrong she did know.
Her persuasion did win—
Back to Rome again.
Four years later, she finished her time here below.

Think what you can learn from this saint and her tale.
How you can apply it to help you prevail.
Then mold what you do
And boldly pursue
Her pattern of holiness. Follow her trail.

Timeline of Events

Year	Event
1270	Marco Polo journeys to China; Phillip III becomes king of France
1274	Death of St. Thomas Aquinas
1291	End of crusades
1309-77	Papacy moved from Rome to Avignon, France, for reign of seven popes (Babylonian Captivity)
1322	Birth of Blessed Imelda Lambertini (died in 1333)
1324	Death of Marco Polo
1328	England acknowledges Scotland's independence
1337-1453	Hundred Years' War between France and England
1345	Aztecs arrive in central Mexico
1347	Birth of St. Catherine of Siena
1347-53	Black Death (Bubonic Plague) sweeps Europe
1353	Catherine's first vision of saints
1359	Catherine cuts her hair and lives as a servant in her parents' home
1361	Black Death reappears in England
1363	Catherine receives the Dominican habit as a tertiary and receives an invisible ring from our Lord (spiritual marriage)
1368	Death of Catherine's father; restoration of the Great Wall of China
1369	John Hus born (died in 1415)
1370	Steel crossbow used in battle
1375	War breaks out between Pope Gregory XI and the Republic of Florence; Catherine acts as dove of peace
1376	Catherine visits Pope Gregory XI in Avignon in the summer; on September 13th, Pope Gregory XI leaves for Rome; John Wycliffe calls for reform in the Church
1377	January 17th, Pope Gregory XI arrives in Rome to end Church's "Babylonian Captivity"
1378-1417	Great Schism begins with election of both Pope Urban VI and Clement VII
1380	Death of St. Catherine of Siena
1387-1400	Geoffrey Chaucer writes "Canterbury Tales"
1396	Birth of Johann Gutenberg, inventor of printing in Europe
1409	Council of Pisa called in attempt to end Great Schism
1412	Birth of St. Joan of Arc
1414	General Council of the Church at Constance, ending Great Schism and reforming the Church; Thomas á Kempis writes Imitation of Christ
1461	Canonization of St. Catherine (declared a Doctor of Church in 1970)

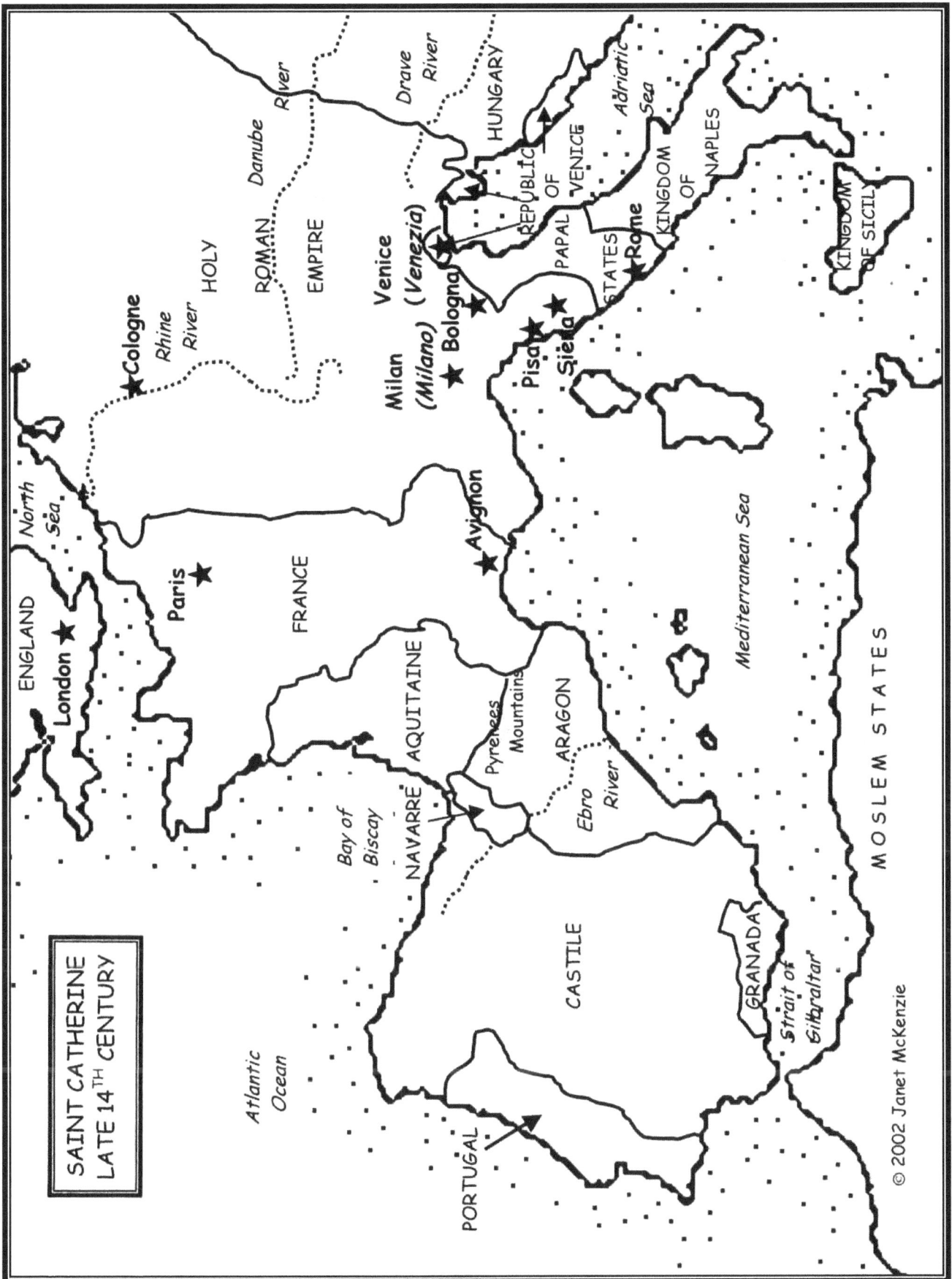

SAINT CATHERINE
LATE 14TH CENTURY

© 2002 Janet McKenzie

Chapter 1—In Which Catherine Sees a Vision of Saints in the Sky

REVIEW Vocabulary

Why are you so *fidgety*   *Dominican*
who was *inclined* to be cross   *vision*

??? Comprehension Questions/Narration Prompts

1.   What did Lapa want for her youngest daughter?
2.   How old was Catherine when she first saw saints in the sky? Who did she see?

Forming Opinions/Drawing Conclusions

1.   What does Lapa's insistence that Catherine and Stefano not stop to visit in the Church tell you about the customary habits of Catherine as a young child?
2.   Explain Catherine's thoughts regarding the difficulty of becoming a saint amidst the noise and bustle of home (page 10). Do you agree? Explain your answer.

Growing in Holiness

Two references are made in this chapter to Jesus in the Blessed Sacrament—the first when Lapa cautions the children not to stop for a visit at the church and the second when Stefano chides Catherine for seeing our Lord above the church when He is in the church. Make more visits to our Lord in the Blessed Sacrament to pray. Remember His presence whenever you are in church and whenever you receive Him in Holy Communion. If you are not able to visit our Lord in the tabernacle, make frequent spiritual communions with Him. (See note in the answer key on page 59 for more information on making a spiritual communion.)

Timeline Work

Taping sheets of plain paper end-to-end, make a timeline representing the years from 1270 through 1461. Let three inches equal 25 years. Mark on your timeline the dates and events from 1270 through 1353, using information from page 44.

Searching Scripture

1.   Review the shades of the rainbow that Jacopo used as a model for his dyes. Read the story of God's covenant with man as sealed by the sign of the rainbow in Genesis 9:8-17. Read also Sirach 43:12-13 (Ecclesiasticus 43:11-12) regarding the rainbow.
2.   All the saints Catherine saw in the vision are in the Bible. Read in the Bible about these three saints. Why do you think these particular saints appeared to Catherine?

Chapter 2–In Which Catherine Runs Away to Become a Hermit

⟨REVIEW⟩ Vocabulary

in the *cobbled* street   *hermit*
Nearby *hovered* a guardian angel   *saint*

⁇ Comprehension Questions/Narration Prompts

1. Why did Catherine decide to run away from home?
2. What did our Lord tell Catherine that her life's work was to be?
3. When she decided to return home, Catherine prayed. How quickly was her prayer answered and in what way?
4. Why did Stefano find it hard to believe all that Catherine told him?

💡 Forming Opinions/Drawing Conclusions

List three activities or habits that you can begin (or change) that would help you start becoming a saint in your own home.

✝ Growing in Holiness

We cannot all become hermits and run away whenever we need time with God. Recall that Jesus often went off to be alone with God and pray. Discuss the possibility of the entire family having a day of quiet prayer. Remember to maintain a peaceful atmosphere all day with time for both individual and family prayer. Use candles, soft music, and incense to create a more prayerful atmosphere.

🗺 Geography

Trace the map on page 45 of this study guide. Color these seas and oceans blue: Atlantic, North, Adriatic, and Mediterranean as well as these rivers: Rhine, Danube, Ebro, and Drave. The remainder of the map will be completed in Chapter 7.

✓ Checking the Catechism

Older students may read text paragraphs 897-933, 1593, 1597, and 1660 (188-193, 325, and 535) in the *Catechism of the Catholic Church* (*CCC*) on the vocations of lay people and the consecrated life. If desired, complete Activity #55 in *100* Activities. Remember to pray daily to discern God's unique plan for you.

📖 Searching Scripture

1. Re-read the conversation between Stefano and Catherine found on page 17. Then read Matthew 13:57. Why is it hard to believe that saints and prophets live among us?
2. John the Baptist lived alone in the desert—Matthew 3:1-6. Also read about St. Paul's three years in the desert in Galatians 1:15-18.

Chapter 3–In Which Catherine Takes Drastic Measures to Avoid Marriage

---

⧉ Vocabulary
daughter's *cropped* head   *mercy*
not inclined to hold a *grudge*   *disciples*

⁇⁇ Comprehension Questions/Narration Prompts
1. Relate the story of Catherine's hair and why she cut it.
2. How was Catherine punished for this?
3. What plan did Catherine devise to make her new work more pleasant?

☀ Forming Opinions/Drawing Conclusions
1. Think of how you handled your punishment when disciplined recently. How does your attitude compare with Catherine's attitude toward her punishment?
2. Describe Catherine's plan to think of her family as the Holy Family of Nazareth. How can you incorporate this plan into your daily living?
3. Christians are often criticized for having "odd ideas"—such as not caring about money, personal looks, or powerful positions. Do you think it was wrong that Catherine did not wish to marry and help her family financially? Explain your answer.

▣ For Further Study
The church in Siena was a Dominican church; Catherine's stepbrother, Father Thomas della Fonte, was a Dominican priest. Research the history of the Dominican order, which was a relatively new order at the time of Catherine's life.

✝ Growing in Holiness
While Catherine's punishment may seem severe, you can do much in your family to help out without becoming a Cinderella. Do at least two chores around the house each day without being asked. Offer them up to Jesus in reparation for sins. Be sure not to seek any praise, reward, or even recognition for these acts.

✓ Checking the Catechism
Older students may read text paragraphs 2197-2207 (455-458) in the *CCC* on the domestic church. If desired, complete Activity #57 in *100 Activities*.

▥ Searching Scripture
While there is not much information on the life of the Holy Family in the Bible, you can read of Jesus' submission to His parents in Luke 2:41-52.

Chapter 4—In Which St. Dominic Appears to Catherine

✖REVIEW✖ Vocabulary

in the *somber* black   *religious orders*
saw each one of them *beckon* to her   *religious family*

??? Comprehension Questions/Narration Prompts

1. The second time Catherine saw saints in the sky she recognized more of them. Name the six saints she saw.
2. What was the message that St. Dominic gave to Catherine?

💡 Forming Opinions/Drawing Conclusions

1. Why do you think God allowed Jacopo to see the dove above his daughter when he found her at prayer?
2. What you think is God's plan for Catherine's life? Quote statements from the book to support your argument.

📖 For Further Study

Briefly research each of the six saints in Catherine's vision. Review how each of them is portrayed in pictures so that you too might recognize them.

✝ Growing in Holiness

Jocopo found Catherine kneeling in her room praying just as Jesus has asked us to pray (Matthew 6:6) and just as Daniel prayed in Daniel 6:11 (6:10-11). "Her heart was full of gratitude" (page 27). Remember when you pray to not just use the most common form of prayer—petition or asking God for various things—but also to use the other four forms of prayer: adoration of God, intercession or praying for others, thanksgiving, and praise of God. Try to make your prayers less asking and more thanking, praising, and thinking of others.

🗓 Timeline Work

Add the dates and events from 1359 through 1370 to your timeline.

✓ Checking the Catechism

Older students can read text paragraphs 222-27, 795, 1167, 1328, and 2637-38 (43, 67, 221, 443, 547, 550, and 555) in the *CCC* on giving thanks. If desired, complete Activity #66 in *100 Activities*. Read too the citations in the *CCC* from St. Catherine's *Dialogue* in text paragraphs 313, 356, and 1937.

Chapter 5–In Which Catherine Receives the Dominican Habit

⭐REVIEW⭐ Vocabulary

in this tiny *chamber*

a *smallpox* plague

Tertiary

Ash Wednesday

??? Comprehension Questions/Narration Prompts

1. At the age of sixteen, what did Catherine decide her life work was to be? What did she do because of this decision?
2. Catherine needed her mother in order to implement the second step of her plan. What did she request her mother to do? Did her mother agree to do it?
3. What did God do to help Catherine in her plan to become a Dominican tertiary?
4. What did Catherine predict regarding her mother's future?
5. Who taught Catherine to read and write?
6. What saints did Catherine see in her third vision?
7. What did our Lord say to Catherine when He placed the invisible ring on her finger? How old was Catherine?

Forming Opinions/Drawing Conclusions

What does "a religious with the whole world for her convent" (page 36) mean?

For Further Study

Briefly research each of the five saints of Catherine's third vision. Be sure to find pictures of each saint so that you can recognize their faces.

Growing in Holiness

Catherine speaks of her life's work—suffering for sinners and their sins. Think of a sinner from the news or from your own life and offer all of your sacrifices for the next week for this person. Offer prayers, fast from a certain food or pleasure, make visits to Jesus in the tabernacle, and do extra chores.

✓ Checking the Catechism

Older students should read in the CCC text paragraphs 1434-38, 2041-43, 2174-76, and 2180-88 (241, 276, 289, 291, 301, 432, 450-454, 567) regarding two of the commandments of the Church—our obligation regarding Sunday Mass and the Church's laws on fasting.

Searching Scripture

"The prophet David began to play sweet music on his little harp" (page 39). Read the beginning of the story of David in 1 Samuel (Kings) 16:11-18:5.

Chapter 6–In Which Catherine Tends to the Sick and Converts Sinners

✖REVIEW✖ Vocabulary

go into *rapture* for joy   *sanctifying grace*
die on the *gallows*   *Purgatory*

?? ??? Comprehension Questions/Narration Prompts

1. What did our Lord request of Catherine after giving her the invisible ring?
2. Other than again being the family's servant, what other duties did Catherine assume?
3. Catherine contracted the disease of leprosy while tending the sick. What were her first and second thoughts after being miraculously cured of this disease?
4. What did Catherine's sufferings and prayers for the convicted criminal gain?
5. What offering did Catherine make on behalf of her dying father?

For Further Study

1. Research the disease of leprosy and write a brief report. In addition to general information on the disease itself, be sure to include information such as its current treatment and treatment in Jesus' and Catherine's time, its current rate of occurrence, and its rate of occurrence in both Jesus' and Catherine's time. Is leprosy still an incurable disease? Find two biblical passages which deal with cases of leprosy.
2. Mysticism refers to a state of the soul in which God is known in a way that no human effort could produce. Research the degrees of mystical contemplation—union with God—as outlined by St. Teresa of Avila: the two nights of the soul (sense and spirit) before mystical union, the prayer of quiet, full union, ecstasy, and spiritual marriage or transforming union (as illustrated by Catherine in this chapter). Mysticism is not restricted to a privileged few. God wants every soul to be completely united with Him.

✝ Growing in Holiness

Perform at least three corporal works of mercy and three spiritual works of mercy within the next week.

✓ Checking the Catechism

Older students may review the teachings of the *CCC* on the works of mercy in text paragraph 2447 (520) and the Beatitudes in text paragraphs 1716-29 (359-362). Younger students may review the spiritual and corporal works of mercy, and the Beatitudes in their catechisms. If desired, complete Activity #20 in *100 Activities*.

📖 Searching Scripture

Read Matthew 25:31-46. Also read these passages related to mysticism: Psalm 27 (26): 4-5, Psalm 63 (62), Psalm 73 (72):25-26, 2 Corinthians 3:18, and 1 Peter 1:8.

Chapter 7–In Which Catherine Travels to See the Holy Father

Vocabulary

invasion by the *Turks*

in a kind of *trance*

Vatican

cardinals

Comprehension Questions/Narration Prompts
1. Catherine bore the stigmata of Christ (pierced hands, side, and feet) for five years. At what age did she receive the invisible stigmata of Christ?
2. Why did Catherine decide to travel to Avignon, France—walking if necessary?

Forming Opinions/Drawing Conclusions

1. "A woman's place is in the home" (page 52). Comment on this statement considering Catherine's vocation as given to her by our Lord.
2. Catherine asked that wise words be put in her mouth whenever she met sinners so that she could bring them to God. What "wise words" would you say to convert sinners?

For Further Study
1. Research the Papal Palace in Avignon, France. How many years did the popes reside there? Which popes resided there? Why were they there?
2. Research the political climate at this time. Study the Turks and their invasion of the European continent at this time. Where were they from? What did they wish to accomplish? Why did they hate the Christians? What is the "terrible war" that is mentioned at the beginning of Chapter 8?

Growing in Holiness
If it has been more than a month since your last reception of the Sacrament of Penance (Confession), plan on participating in this sacrament within the next two weeks.

Geography
Complete the map started in Chapter 2 by labeling the cities red and the countries green. On the map provided, cities are indicated with a star, and countries are in capital letters. Using a modern map, find the current country to which each city now belongs.

Checking the Catechism
Priests followed Catherine around as she instilled contrition and the need to go to confession in many people. Older students may read these text paragraphs in the *CCC*: 980, 1422, 1440, and 1448-49 (200 and 296-311) on the Sacrament of Penance while younger students review this topic in their own catechisms. Complete Activity #90 in *100 Activities*.

Chapter 8–In Which Catherine Persuades the Holy Father to Return the Papacy to Rome

REVIEW Vocabulary

cloaks of *ermine*   *pope*
he saw that Catherine *winced*   *catechism*

??? Comprehension Questions/Narration Prompts
1. Why did Catherine feel that the Holy Father should return to Rome?
2. Other than talk to the Holy Father (Pope Gregory XI), what else did Catherine do in her efforts to get the pope to return to Rome?
3. What convinced Pope Gregory XI to return to Rome?

Forming Opinions/Drawing Conclusions
Why did Catherine not want the Holy Father to see the wounds of Christ on her hands?

For Further Study
Research the pontificate of Gregory XI, who reigned as pope from January 1371 to March 1378. At the urging of Catherine, he left Avignon in September 1376 but did not arrive in Rome until January 1377. Find out why.

Growing in Holiness
As Catherine prayed to the Holy Spirit when she had a difficult task ahead of her, so too must we pray for the Holy Spirit's guidance in our lives. Ask for the assistance of the Holy Spirit whenever you are unsure about what to do or say. It may be a simple aspiration such as "Come. Holy Spirit, come." Pray too that our pope will always be guided by the Holy Spirit.

✓ Checking the Catechism
Catherine talks of Rome as the city of St. Peter, the first pope. Younger students should study the offices of pope and bishop as well as the mission of the apostles in their catechisms. Older students may read text paragraphs 857-62 (174-176 and 179-187) in the *CCC* on the apostolic Church. If desired, complete Activity #48 in *100 Activities*.

Searching Scripture
Read Matthew 28:19-20. This mission to teach and baptize was given to the apostles and may have been part of the message that Catherine gave to Gregory XI. Also read Matthew 16:13-20 regarding our first pope.

Chapter 9–In Which Catherine's Suffering Ends

REVIEW Vocabulary
Catherine *beseeched* Our Lord   *Last Sacraments*

??? Comprehension Questions/Narration Prompts
1. What two promises did Jesus make to Catherine regarding her family?
2. Why did Catherine think of herself a failure?
3. In what important aspect was Catherine not a failure?

Forming Opinions/Drawing Conclusions
Applying what you have learned about St. Catherine in this book, explain the accomplishments, attitudes, or habits that contributed to her canonization as a saint.

For Further Study
1. Research the procedure for electing a pope. Include the changes made in the eleventh century, those made by the Third Council of the Lateran in 1179, and those made in 1975 by Pope Paul VI. Who is eligible to become pope? Determine who nominates and who votes. Can the pope be removed from office or resign? (Use Laux's *Church History*, Johnson's *The Story of the Church*, or search the Internet.)
2. St. Catherine's holiness and learning—as displayed in her life and her *Dialogue*—prompted the Church to confer upon her the honorary title of "Doctor of the Church" in 1970. Read more about the Doctors of the Catholic Church on page 56 below. What other saints in the Windeatt biography series have been given this title? Research the life of one of the Church's Doctors.

Growing in Holiness
Memorize one or more of the following aspirations to be recited after receiving Holy Communion: "O Jesus in the Blessed Sacrament, have mercy on us." "Eucharistic Heart of Jesus, increase my faith, hope, and love." "Sacred Heart of Jesus, may You be known, may You be loved, may You be imitated." "Heart of Jesus burning with love for me, inflame my heart with love for Thee." "O my God and my all, may the sweet flame of Your love consume my soul, that I may die to the world for the love of You, who has died on the Cross for love of me."

Timeline Work
Add the events from 1375 through 1461 to complete your timeline.

Searching Scripture
Regarding Catherine's inedia (ability to live on the Eucharist as the sole source of food and drink), read John 4:31-34. Also read John 6:48-59.

Doctors of the Catholic Church

The title of "Doctor of the Church", a title originally conferred on the four great Western Fathers of the Church—Gregory the Great, Ambrose, Augustine, and Jerome—is bestowed upon those canonized saints of the Church whose writing and/or preaching is outstanding in guiding the faithful. The Doctors of the Church are recognized for their learning and holiness of life. Listed below are the Doctors, the dates they lived, and the year they were given the title of "Doctor of the Church."

1. St. Athanasius – c. 297-373 (prior to 750)
2. St. Ephrem or Ephraem of Syria – c. 306-c. 373 (1920)
3. St. Cyril of Jerusalem – c. 315-386 (1882)
4. St. Hilary of Poitiers – c. 315-c. 368 (1851)
5. St. Gregory Nazianzen or Gregory of Nazianzus – c. 329-c. 389 (prior to 750)
6. St. Basil the Great – c. 329-379 (prior to 750)
7. St. Ambrose – c. 340–397 (prior to 750)
8. St. Jerome – c. 342-c. 420 (prior to 750)
9. St. John Chrysostom – c. 347-407 (prior to 750)
10. St. Augustine – 354-430 (prior to 750)
11. St. Cyril of Alexandria – c. 376-444 (1882)
12. Pope St. Leo the Great – c. 400-461 (1574)
13. St. Peter Chrysologus – c. 406 –c. 450 (1729)
14. Pope St. Gregory the Great - c. 540-604 (prior to 750)
15. St. Isidore of Seville – c. 560-636 (1722)
16. St. Bede the Venerable – c. 673-735 (1899)
17. St. John Damascene or John of Damascus) – c. 676-c. 749 (1890)
18. St. Peter Damian – c. 1007-1072 (1828)
19. St. Anselm of Canterbury– 1033-1109 (1720)
20. St. Bernard of Clairvaux – c. 1090-1153 (1830)
21. St. Anthony of Padua – 1195-1231 (1946)
22. St. Albert the Great – c. 1206-1280 (1931)
23. St. Bonaventure – c. 1221-1274 (1588)
24. St. Thomas Aquinas – c. 1225-1274 (1568)
25. St. Catherine of Siena – 1347-1380 (1970)
26. St. Teresa of Avila – 1515-1582 (1970)
27. St. Peter Canisius – 1521-1597 (1925)
28. St. Robert Bellarmine – 1542-1621 (1931)
29. St. John of the Cross – 1542-1591 (1926)
30. St. Lawrence of Brindisi – 1559-1619 (1959)
31. St. Francis de Sales – 1567-1622 (1877)
32. St. Alphonsus Liguori – 1696-1787 (1871)
33. St. Therese of Lisieux – 1873-1897 (1997)

Book Summary Test for *Saint Catherine of Siena*

Directions: Answer in complete sentences. If necessary, use the back of the page for additional writing space. 100 possible points, 20 points for each answer.

1. Name at least three miracles attributed to Catherine in her lifetime.

   _____

   _____

   _____

2. To what religious order did Catherine belong?

   _____

   _____

3. Describe the daily life of Catherine in her late teens and twenties.

   _____

   _____

   _____

4. What did Catherine accomplish when she traveled to France?

   _____

   _____

   _____

5. St. Catherine of Siena shows us that it is not necessary to become a priest or cloistered nun to achieve holiness. How can we become holy even in the midst of the distractions of daily family life? What habits are important? What information and practices will aid in our quest to increase our holiness?

   _____

   _____

Saint Catherine Siena, The Story of the Girl Who Saw Saints in the Sky
Answer Key to Comprehension Questions

Chapter 1—In Which Catherine Sees a Vision of Saints in the Sky
1. Lapa wanted Catherine to grow up to be beautiful and marry a rich man, so Lapa and her husband could enlarge their shop.
2. Catherine was six when she first saw a vision of saints in the sky. She recognized Christ the King and some of the others as John the Baptist, St. Peter, and St. Paul.

Growing In Holiness

The Council of Trent, held in the sixteenth century, asked all the faithful to make a spiritual communion on the days that they do not receive Holy Communion. St. Alphonsus Liguori advises us to make a spiritual communion at least three times a day—in the morning, at noon, and in the evening. Our Lord appeared to Sister Benigna Consolata of Como, Italy, in 1916 and said, "Make as many spiritual communions as possible to supply for the many sacramental communions which are not made. One every quarter of an hour is not enough. Make them shorter, but more numerous." One spiritual communion prayer follows: "My Jesus, I believe that You are present in the Most Holy Eucharist. I love You above all things, and I desire to receive You into my soul. Since I cannot at this moment receive You sacramentally, come at least spiritually into my heart. I embrace You as if You were already here and unite myself wholly to You. Never permit me to be separated from You." You may also memorize a shorter form—"I believe that You are in the most holy Sacrament. I love You and desire You. Come into my heart. I embrace You; never leave me!" Alternatively, memorize a spiritual communion prayer of your own creation.

Chapter 2—In Which Catherine Runs Away to Become a Hermit
1. Catherine felt she could not be a saint among the hustle and bustle of her home, so she decided to run away and become a hermit in a cave.
2. Jesus told Catherine that her life's work was to live in the world and bring others to Christ. Jesus told her that He has need of saints who live in families.
3. Catherine's prayer was answered immediately as she miraculously traveled from the cave to her home instantaneously.
4. As Stefano didn't feel Catherine was capable of walking that far out into the country, he didn't believe the rest of her story either. He also did not believe that miracles were happening to Catherine as he saw her as a very ordinary person—his sister.

Chapter 3—In Which Catherine Takes Measures to Avoid Marriage
1. When she reached the age of twelve, Catherine's parents begin to speak to her about marriage. Catherine did not want to marry as she wished to live alone with God for her entire life. So Catherine went to see her stepbrother, a Dominican priest, for advice. He suggested that she cut off her hair to make herself unattractive. Catherine did as he suggested even though he told her that her parents would be furious.
2. Catherine was given all the jobs of the servant girl as punishment for the hair cutting.
3. Catherine's plan was to think of her father as St. Joseph, her mother as the Blessed Mother, and her brothers and sisters as our Lord's disciples. All the work she did for her family was now done for her heavenly family.

Chapter 4—In Which St. Dominic Appears to Catherine
1. In her second vision of saints, Catherine saw Sts. Benedict, Francis of Assisi, Augustine, Norbert, Bernard, and Dominic.

2. St. Dominic approached Catherine with the habit of his order in his arms and told her that one day she would wear this habit.

Chapter 5—In Which Catherine Receives the Dominican Habit

1. At the age of sixteen, Catherine decided that her life work was to pray and suffer for sinners. She requested the smallest room in the house and decided to confine herself to this room, leaving only to go to Mass and Confession.
2. Catherine requested that her mother go to the Dominicans to ask on her behalf that Catherine be admitted as a Dominican tertiary. Her mother refused to go.
3. God allowed Catherine to become very ill with smallpox in order to fulfill His Holy Will.
4. Catherine predicted that her mother would someday become a Dominican tertiary too.
5. Our Lord Himself miraculously taught Catherine to read and write.
6. The third time Catherine had a vision of saints she saw the Blessed Virgin, St. John the Evangelist, St. Paul, King David, and St. Dominic.
7. When He placed the invisible ring upon her finger, Our Lord said to Catherine, "I take you for my own chosen one" (page 39). Catherine was nineteen years old.

Chapter 6—In Which Catherine Tends to the Sick and Converts Sinners

1. Our Lord asked Catherine to go back to live with her family—no longer to live by herself in her room but to go back into the world.
2. Catherine began to go out to help the sick and the poor by bringing them clothes and food, and nursing them if they were ill.
3. Catherine's first thought after her cure was to thank God for His goodness. Secondly, she was grateful that she could no longer pass the disease to her family.
4. Because of Catherine's suffering and prayers, the criminal agreed to see a priest and go to Confession before his death. She saved his soul from hell.
5. Catherine agreed to bear herself any suffering her father should have had, which then allowed him to go straight to heaven. Catherine suffered pain the rest of her life because of this agreement.

Chapter 7—In Which Catherine Travels to See the Holy Father

1. Catherine received the stigmata of Christ at the age of twenty-eight.
2. Catherine decided to go to Avignon to persuade the pope to return to Rome, a cause started by St. Bridget of Sweden in 1367. (Note: From 1309-1377—throughout the leadership of seven popes—the papacy was in Avignon, France, rather than Rome. This period of sixty-eight years is known as the Avignon Captivity or the Babylonian Captivity—as it was for the same length of time as the exile of the Jewish people in Babylon from 605 BC to 537 BC.)

Chapter 8—In Which Catherine Persuades the Holy Father to Return the Papacy to Rome

1. Catherine felt that Rome was where the pope belonged, as for hundreds of years it was the city of the papacy. Since 1375, the Republic of Florence was at war with Pope Gregory XI. Catherine was hopeful that the pope's return to Rome would help bring peace and save lives.
2. In her attempt to get the pope to return to Rome, Catherine prayed and made sacrifices. She wrote long letters to the pope.
3. Catherine's humility when she spoke to the pope, her statement that it was not she but God who urged him to return, and his confirmation of her stigmata all helped convince Gregory XI that that he should return to Rome.

Chapter 9—In Which Catherine's Suffering Ends

1. Jesus promised Catherine that no one in her house would go to hell and that her mother would not be taken from this world against her own will (unprepared).
2. Due to Catherine's urging, Pope Gregory XI returned to Rome, only to die two years later. After his death, two elections were held to replace him, and two popes claimed to be the true pope—a Frenchman and an Italian. Many people felt that if Catherine had not urged Pope Gregory to return to Rome, the double election never would have taken place. Catherine as-

sumed the responsibility for this decision and viewed herself as a failure because of it. (This event in our Church's history is known as the Great Schism and lasted until 1414.)

3. Catherine had always done the most important thing—she had always loved God and carried out His Holy Will, with no heed to the cost.

Answer Key to Book Summary Test

1. Miracles attributed to Catherine in her lifetime include the following: at least three visions of our Lord and the saints, her hearing the voice of our Lord, the elevation of Catherine above the ground in the cave, the rapid transportation of Catherine home after her day of being a hermit, the appearance of the dove above her head while she was at prayer, the teaching of reading and writing to Catherine by our Lord, the vision in which our Lord gave a wedding ring to her, the appearance of our Lord to Catherine in her room to speak to her about her mission, her cure of leprosy, the demonstration to her of the beauty of a soul in the state of sanctifying grace, the appearance of the stigmata on Catherine, her ability to live without drink or food other than Holy Communion, her ability to persuade Pope Gregory XI to return the papacy to Rome, the return of Lapa from the dead due to Catherine's intercession, and the prophecy of Catherine of the time of her own death.

2. Catherine belonged to the order of the Dominicans as a tertiary or lay Dominican.

3. The daily life of Catherine in her late teens and twenties consisted of much prayer and seclusion with many corporal works of mercy within her home and throughout the community. She spent three years (from the ages of sixteen to nineteen) within the confines of her bedroom at home praying and offering sacrifices for sinners, only coming out to attend Mass and receive the other sacraments. From the age of nineteen to her death at the age of thirty-three, she performed works of mercy—spiritual and corporal—caring for the sick, visiting those in prison, bringing food to the hungry, and causing many to return to the Faith through the Sacrament of Penance or Reconciliation.

4. When she traveled to France, St. Catherine of Siena finished the work started by St. Bridget and many others by persuading Pope Gregory XI to return to Rome—thus ending the sixty-eight-year pontifical reign in Avignon, France.

5. Answers will vary.

Study Guide for

*The Miraculous Medal,
The Story of Our Lady's
Appearances to
Saint Catherine Labouré*

St. Catherine Labouré

Zoe Catherine Labouré in France was born.
At nine when her mom died, Catherine did mourn.
With Mary as aid,
She was not afraid.
Her hard work she offered to Jesus each morn.

At twelve she felt called to leave for the convent.
Her father, however, refused his consent.
She fasted and prayed
While at home she stayed.
Eleven years she waited, but not quite content.

Called by St. Vincent to follow his lead,
She entered his order to help those in need.
The habit she wore—
As she had hoped for—
A Daughter of Charity in dress, word, and deed.

She worked in the kitchen and laundry room too.
No job was too humble for Catherine to do.
No one connected—
Nor even suspected—
Her part in the Medal. No one had a clue.

Then her vision of Mary became the mold.
Soon millions of medals were cast and were sold.
Its power was great,
Which helped illustrate,
That Mary, our mother, no grace will withhold.

Her visions of Mary two ways were portrayed—
A medal to be worn and a statue displayed.
One shows her grace,
The other her place.
Mary pleads for the world, God's mercy to sway.

Think what you can learn from this saint and her tale.
How you can apply it to help you prevail.
Then mold what you do
And boldly pursue
Her pattern of holiness. Follow her trail.

Timeline of Events

Year	Event
1776-83	American Revolutionary War fought
1789	French Revolution begins (to 1799); John Carroll named Bishop of Baltimore
1799	Pauline Marie Jaricot born on July 22nd in Lyons, France; Napoleon Bonaparte comes to power in France
1803	President Jefferson secures the Louisiana Purchase for the United States
1806	Birth of Zoe Catherine Labouré on May 2nd
1809	Napoleon Bonaparte takes possession of the Papal States (until 1815); St. Elizabeth Seton establishes Sisters of Charity in Emmitsburg, Maryland
1815	Death of Catherine's mother; Catherine takes Mary as her mother; Battle of Waterloo; French monarchy re-established
1817	Death of Jane Austen, English author of *Pride and Prejudice*
1818	Catherine feels call to religious life at the age of twelve
1830	First apparition of the Blessed Virgin to Catherine on July 18th; second apparition on November 27th; death of Simon Bolivar
1831	In January, Catherine makes her religious vows and receives the habit of the Daughters of Charity; invention of the telegraph by Joseph Henry
1832	First Miraculous Medal made
1834	Over six million Miraculous Medals distributed
1836	Founding of the Association of the Children of Mary on December 8th; Texas gains independence from Mexico
1837	Queen Victoria begins reign in England; Samuel Morse invents the Morse code
1841	St. John Bosco ordained a priest
1842	Conversion of Alphonse Ratisbonne in Rome on January 20th
1845	Conversion of John Henry Newman; Irish famine begins (continues until 1850)
1846	Apparition at La Salette, France, on September 19th
1847	The Children of Mary canonically established by Pope Pius IX
1850	Charles Dickens writes *David Copperfield*
1854	Doctrine of the Immaculate Conception proclaimed
1858	Apparition in Lourdes, France, of our Lady to Bernadette Soubirous
1859	Death of St. John Vianney in August
1861	Beginning of the United States Civil War
1862	Pauline Jaricot dies in Lyons, France, on January 9th
1865	Death of Father Aladel on April 25th; end of the United States Civil War
1867	Japanese Shogunate abolished; barbed wire invented in the United States
1869-70	First Vatican Council meets
1870-71	Franco-Prussian War; Stanley meets Livingstone at Lake Tanganyika, Africa
1871	Rebels force the Daughters of Charity to leave Enghien for Toulouse in April; sisters return in May; Great Chicago fire
1875	Alexander Graham Bell makes the first telephone call
1876	Catherine confides her role in the Miraculous Medal to her mother superior and dies on December 31st; over one billion medals distributed
1907	Catherine Labouré declared venerable; beatified on May 28, 1933; and canonized on August 27, 1947

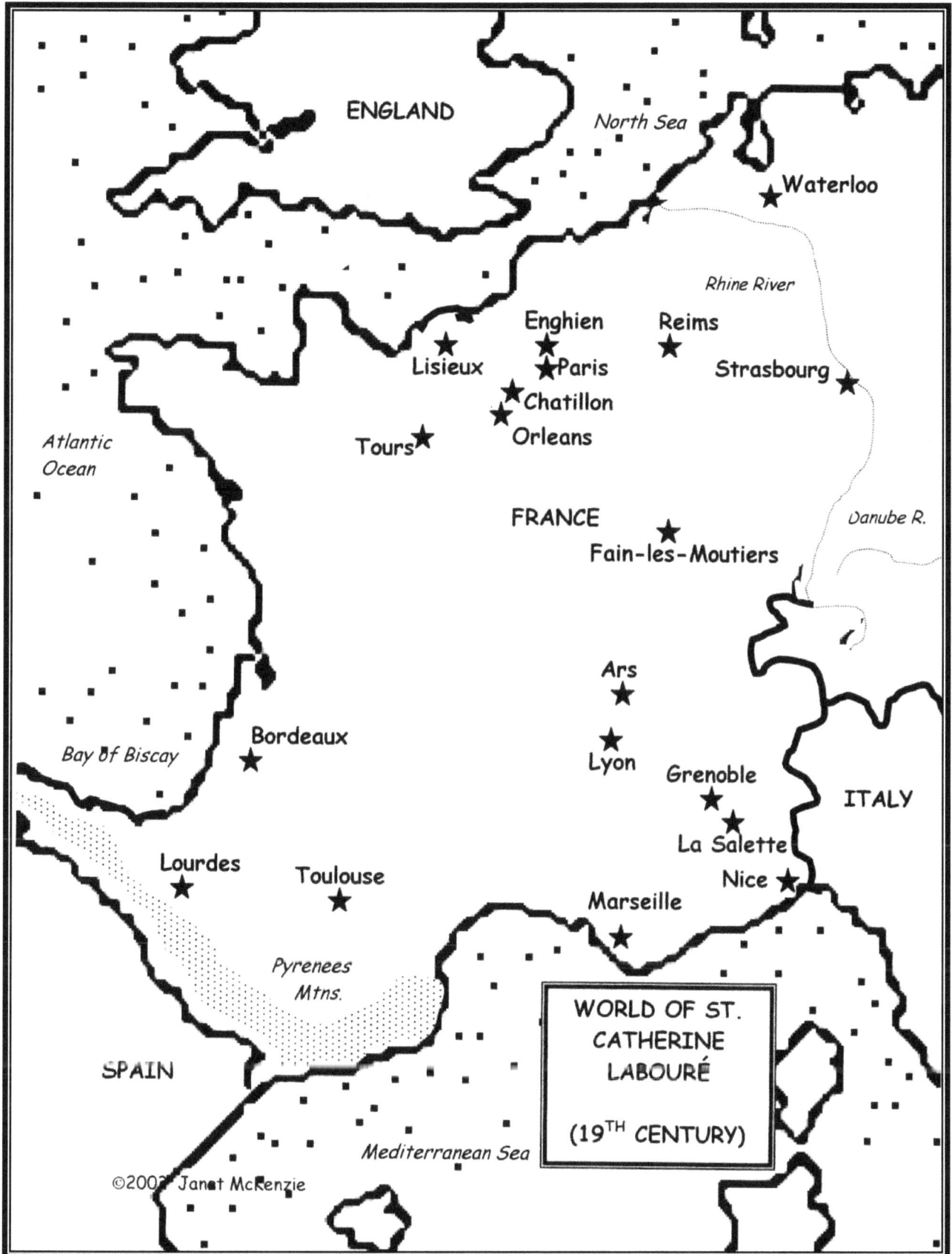

ENGLAND

North Sea

★ Waterloo

Rhine River

Enghien ★ Reims
★ ★
Lisieux Paris
★ ★ Strasbourg
Chatillon ★
★
★ Orleans
Tours ★

Atlantic Ocean

FRANCE
★
Fain-les-Moutiers

Danube R.

Ars
★

★
Lyon

Grenoble
★
★
La Salette

ITALY

Bay Of Biscay

Bordeaux
★

Nice ★

Lourdes Toulouse
★ ★ Marseille
★

Pyrenees Mtns.

SPAIN

WORLD OF ST.
CATHERINE
LABOURÉ

(19TH CENTURY)

Mediterranean Sea

©200? Janet McKenzie

Revision of the Church Calendar and Celebration of the Feasts of the Saints

In Mary Fabyan Windeatt's *The Miraculous Medal, The Story of Our Lady's Appearances to Saint Catherine Labouré*, copyrighted in 1950, Sister Labouré receives the first vision of our Lady on the eve of the "feast of St. Vincent de Paul"—July 18, 1830. The astute reader will note that the Feast of St. Vincent de Paul is now commemorated on September 17th, the day on which St. Vincent de Paul died in 1660 at the age of 80 in Paris, France. This change took place after the Second Vatican Council when the Church's liturgical calendar was assessed and completely reorganized. The Council stressed the inclusion within the liturgical calendar of "days devoted to the memory of the martyrs and the other saints. Raised up to perfection by the manifold grace of God, and already in possession of eternal salvation, they sing God's perfect praise in heaven and offer prayers for us. By celebrating the passage of these saints from earth to heaven the Church proclaims the paschal mystery as achieved in the saints who have suffered and been glorified with Christ; she proposes them to the faithful as examples who draw all to the Father through Christ, and through their merits she pleads for God's favors." (*Constitution on the Sacred Liturgy*)

"The liturgical year is to be revised so that the traditional customs and discipline of the sacred seasons can be preserved or restored to meet the conditions of modern times; their specific character is to be retained so that they duly nourish the piety of the faithful who celebrate the mysteries of Christian redemption, and above all the paschal mystery. . . . Throughout the year the entire mystery of Christ is unfolded, the birthdays (days of death) of the saints are commemorated." (*Constitution on the Sacred Liturgy*)

On May 9, 1969, Pope Paul VI gave his approval for a complete reorganization of the Church calendar; the new calendar went into effect on January 1, 1970. In 1972 the bishops of the United States and many other countries ordered the new calendar into effect; usage became complete with the introduction of the *Sacramentary* in 1974. (*The Catholic Encyclopedia* by Robert Broderick, 1987)

"The highest class of liturgical celebration is the Solemnity (formerly the First Class feast). There are three, among celebrations of saints' days: Joseph, Peter and Paul, John the Baptist.

"The next class consists of Feasts (formerly Second Class feasts). Saints' days celebrated as feasts are those of the apostles, Paul, Mark, Luke, Stephen, Lawrence.

"Memorials are former Third Class feasts. About one third of the saints' days are obligatory memorials, i.e. they must be celebrated unless superseded by a higher ranking celebration (e.g., a day of Lent). The other celebrations of saints' days are optional." (*Saint of the Day* by Leonard Foley, O.F.M., 1975)

Chapters 1 through 3—In Which the Blessed Virgin Appears to Sister Labouré and Gives Her a Special Mission

REVIEW Vocabulary

God wishes to *charge* you with a mission   *altar rail*
. . . they *enveloped* the Blessed Virgin   *meditation*

??? Comprehension Questions/Narration Prompts

1. How was Sister Labouré awakened on the night of July 18, 1830?
2. Who was the little boy who accompanied Sister Labouré?
3. In November, how did Sister Labouré "hear" the voice of the Blessed Virgin?
4. What was the mission—the special work for souls—given to Sister Labouré?

Forming Opinions/Drawing Conclusions

1. Summarize each of the Blessed Virgin's messages to Sister Labouré.
2. Why do you suppose that Father Aladel was reluctant to believe Sister Labouré?

For Further Study

The Blessed Virgin predicted that "dreadful times were in store for France" (page 7). Less than two weeks later, the July Revolution of 1830 occurred in Paris. Research this event as well as the roles played by both Charles X and Louis-Phillipe.

Growing in Holiness

"In time of trial, come here before the altar and pour out all your troubles. Then you will receive every consolation" (page 6). Put the Blessed Virgin Mary's advice into effect within the next week. Make this practice a regular habit.

Timeline Work

Taping sheets of plain paper end-to-end, make a timeline representing the years from 1776 through 1907. Let three inches equal 25 years. Mark on your timeline the dates and events from 1776 through 1830, using information from page 64 of this study guide.

Searching Scripture

"Fear not," said the Blessed Virgin to Sister Labouré (page 6). Many times in Scripture we are told to not be afraid. Read some of these passages in Genesis 15:1, Joshua (Josue) 1:9, Daniel 10:12 and 19, Matthew 10:28 and 31, Matthew 17:7, Matthew 28:5, Luke 1:13 & 30, Luke 2:10, and John 6:20.

Chapters 4 through 6–In Which Sister Labouré Receives the Habit of a Daughter of Charity, and the Bishop Agrees to Begin Work on the Medal

---

✖✱REVIEW✱ Vocabulary

It's *beyond* me   *novitiate*
waited with *bated* breath   *Motherhouse*

??? Comprehension Questions/Narration Prompts

1. What prayer was Sister Labouré directed to place on the medal?
2. To what order was Sister Labouré admitted? What was to be her new name in the religious life? What is the work of this order?
3. What made Father Aladel decide to see the archbishop about the medal as proposed by Sister Catherine?

Forming Opinions/Drawing Conclusions

1. Father Aladel advised Sister Labouré: "Forget the whole thing. Just say your prayers and try to be like the other Sisters. After all, aren't you just a novice?" (page 16). Why would he give her this kind of advice?
2. How many visions or contacts with the Blessed Virgin has Sister Catherine had so far? Did she report them all to the convent chaplain, Father Aladel?

For Further Study

In both the original (Grail Publications) and reprinted (Tan Books and Publishers, Inc.) editions of this book, each chapter begins with an illumination—a miniature illustration or decoration. Research illuminations; when and where did they originate? What was their original purpose? Try your hand at drawing illuminations for your own initials.

Growing in Holiness

Father Aladel describes Sister Catherine as "cheerful, hard-working, obedient, trustworthy . . ." (page 17) and "humble, prayerful, hard-working, obedient . . ." (page 24). Choose one of these traits (the one that describes you the *least*) and firmly resolve to acquire that virtue. Each morning ask for God's grace to practice that virtue. Each night make a sincere examination of conscience to check your progress. Invoke St. Catherine's help whenever tempted to sin against this virtue.

Geography

Trace the map from page 65 of this study guide. Label and color the four seas and oceans blue as well as the two rivers. Label the Pyrenees Mountains and color them brown. (The remaining map will be completed in Chapters 16-18.)

Chapters 7 through 9—In Which the Medal Is Made, Distributed, and Named "Miraculous"

✦REVIEW✦ Vocabulary

golden ball *surmounted* with a cross   *blessing*
preserved from the *cholera* plague   *infirmary*

??? Comprehension Questions/Narration Prompts

1. Explain what the rays extending from our Lady's hands on the medal signify?
2. What are the stipulations for the great graces that abound from the medal?
3. What prompted the title "Miraculous" to become attached to this medal?
4. When did Catherine take the Blessed Virgin for her mother? How did Mary take care of Catherine?

💡 Forming Opinions/Drawing Conclusions

1. "In this way, they would not be advertising their piety" (page 37). What does this mean? Why might you want or not want to "advertise your piety"? In what ways can piety be "advertised"?
2. What are the implications of dying "without the sacraments" (page 40)?
3. What do you suppose is the significance of the reoccurring image of the priest to Sister Catherine in her youth? Speculate who this priest might be.

✝ Growing in Holiness

Sister Catherine prayed and made sacrifices for John, even secretly placing a medal under his mattress. Find someone in your neighborhood, parish, or family in need of prayers and/or conversion. Devise a plan detailing how you might reach this person. Imitate Sister Catherine by executing this plan, sacrificing and praying for this person. Be sure to include the Miraculous Medal prayer in your service plan: "O Mary, conceived without sin, pray for us who have recourse to thee." Read and live Colossians 1:9-13.

✓ Checking the Catechism

Sister Catherine described her life before entering the religious community. Older students may read text paragraphs 2197-2210 (456-462) in the *Catechism of the Catholic Church (CCC)* to better understand the family as the foundation of society. Younger students may study the model of the Holy Family in their own catechisms. If desired, complete Activity #56 in *100 Activities Based on the Catechism of the Catholic Church*.

📖 Searching Scripture

Relate at least one incident from the Old Testament and one from the New Testament that concern dreams. Find the specific passages that relate these events. While God can speak to us through dreams, does that mean that every dream is a message from God? Explain your answer.

Chapters 10 through 12–In Which Old John Is Converted, and Sister Catherine Shows Father Aladel a Pathway to Heaven

✦REVIEW✦ Vocabulary
adapt herself to her new circumstances   *founded*
at the *threshold* of joy   *spiritual guide*

??? Comprehension Questions/Narration Prompts
1. Who was the priest of Sister Catherine's dreams?
2. For how many years did Sister Catherine prepare to enter the convent of the Daughters of Charity? How did she prepare?
3. What did Sister Catherine do to help bring about the conversion of John?

Forming Opinions/Drawing Conclusions
1. Why do you think Sister Catherine's father was opposed to her becoming a nun?
2. Sister Catherine stated that many people pray for "unimportant things" (page 57). What might some of these things be? Give examples from the text of some important things for which to pray. Add other important things relevant to your life.
3. Summarize Catherine's idea that people were meant to be happy as outlined on pages 50-51. Remember each day to make an effort to know God and His Will.
4. State several ideas about prayer that you learned in these chapters. How can you use these ideas to imitate St. Catherine Labouré's prayerful habits?

For Further Study
Research St. Vincent de Paul and the two religious orders that he founded—the Daughters of Charity and the Priests of the Mission.

Growing in Holiness
Catherine implores Father Aladel to "tell people to ask the Blessed Virgin for the grace to love God as she did when she was their age" (page 58). This "perfect act of love . . . could bring even the most ordinary soul straight to heaven." Compose a short prayer that includes these thoughts, and recite it frequently throughout the day.

Timeline Work
Add the dates and events from 1831 through 1854 to your timeline.

Searching Scripture
". . . say 'yes' to what He wanted" (page 50). Find examples in Scripture of those who have said "yes" to God. Include at least two Old Testament characters.

Chapters 13 through 15–In Which the Medal Lives Up to Its Name, and the Association of the Children of Mary Is Founded

✦REVIEW✦ Vocabulary

Storekeepers had *dispatched* . . . medals   *Memorare*
an *obscure* nun   *Jesuit Fathers (Jesuits)*

❓❓❓ Comprehension Questions/Narration Prompts

1. What two desires does John express in chapter 13?
2. What made the sisters at Enghien suspect Sister Catherine of being the nun responsible for the Miraculous Medal? What made them change their mind?
3. With what other group did the Children of Mary wish to become affiliated?

💡 Forming Opinions/Drawing Conclusions

1. When did the first Miraculous Medal appear? By the end of 1834, about how many medals had been distributed? Why were so many of them brass?
2. Why was it important to keep the secret of Catherine's identity?
3. Why were the special blessings of the Holy Father and the attachment of indulgences important in the formation of the Children of Mary?
4. What does "true state of his soul" refer to on page 73? What can we do to better understand the true state of our own souls?

✚ Growing in Holiness

The requirements for children admitted to the Association (or Sodality) of the Children of Mary include the wearing, day and night, of the Miraculous Medal; regular recitation of the rosary, the Litany of Loreto, and the Memorare; and processions and devotional prayers to Mary especially during the month of May. Form an Association of the Children of Mary within your family, neighborhood, or parish. Set up regular meeting dates and outline requirements for membership.

✓ Checking the Catechism

Sister Catherine reassures John that he will make a good confession. Read what the requirements for a good confession are in the *CCC* text paragraphs 1450-60 (302-306). Read too the *CCC* text paragraphs 1467 (309) and 2490 which explain the "seal of confession" as alluded to by Father Aladel on page 65. Younger students may study the Sacrament of Penance or Reconciliation in their own catechisms.

📖 Searching Scripture

"He was just about as prejudiced as Saul of Tarsus against the Christian faith" (page 72). Read the story of Saul in Acts 7:54-8:3 and Acts 9:1-2.

Chapters 16 through 18–In Which War Causes the Daughters of Charity to Leave Enghien, and Our Lady Makes a New Request

✦REVIEW✦ Vocabulary
wealth of heaven escapes in *torrents*   *Immaculate Conception*
convulsed by all sorts of *calamities*   *Article of Faith*

??? Comprehension Questions/Narration Prompts
1. What aspect of the Miraculous Medal was the most special to Sister Catherine?
2. List the three duties of Sister Catherine at the convent at Enghien.
3. Why did the sisters have to leave the Enghien convent in April of 1871?
4. What "new request" bothered Catherine so much that her health was affected?

Forming Opinions/Drawing Conclusions
The apparition of La Salette stresses keeping Sundays holy and refraining from bad language. These two requests refer to which of the Ten Commandments?

For Further Study
How has Sister Catherine's prophesy of the twentieth century as the age of Marian apparitions come true? Using a Catholic encyclopedia or the Internet, research various Marian apparitions that have occurred since the beginning of the twentieth century. Make a chart listing specific *approved* apparitions and their messages.

✝ Growing in Holiness
". . . crown Our Lady's statue in May . . ." (page 88). Begin to honor Mary in your own home each May by decorating a statue of Mary. See page 74 of this study guide to determine what each of the other months, as well as the days of the week, are dedicated to and, as a family, celebrate each day's and month's theme with special activities, prayers, decorations, and processions. Celebrate too the memorials of the Miraculous Medal and St. Catherine Labouré on November 27 and 28.

Geography
Complete the map started in Chapters 4-6 by labeling the cities red and the countries green. On the map provided, cities are indicated with a star, and countries are in bold capitals. Locate Fain-les-Moutiers, the birthplace of St. Catherine.

✓ Checking the Catechism
Older students may read text paragraphs 490-93 (96) and 217 in the *CCC* on the Immaculate Conception, while younger students study this same topic in their own catechisms.

Chapters 19 through 21–In Which Catherine Fulfills Our Lady's Request and Dies in Peace

🔲REVIEW Vocabulary
made a *valiant* effort   *Vincent de Paul (St.)*
procuring the services of a . . . sculptor   *Revelation*

??? Comprehension Questions/Narration Prompts
1. Why did Sister Catherine, who was in ill health, make the uncomfortable trip to Paris to see the convent's confessor, Father Chinchon?
2. After an unsuccessful trip to see Father Chinchon, what did Catherine confide to Mother Superior? What request did she make of her mother superior?
3. For how long had Sister Catherine kept secret her role in the Miraculous Medal?
4. Why was Sister Catherine disappointed in the beautiful statue?
5. What truth did Sister Catherine's life reveal to those who knew her? What "secret of being a saint" did her life make others realize? Who usually knows this secret best of all?

💡 Forming Opinions/Drawing Conclusions
1. Explain the differences between the image of our Lady on the Miraculous Medal and her image on the statue that Sister Catherine commissioned.
2. What can you do to promote devotion to the Miraculous Medal?

📖 For Further Study
From the pictures in the book, study the images of both sides of the medal (pages 14 and 19) as well as the image of the statue as found on page 99. To the best of your ability, draw or trace these images labeling the significance of each of the parts. Spread devotion to the Miraculous Medal by presenting your work to your family or to another group within your neighborhood or parish.

✝ Growing in Holiness
"It's really the children who can teach the rest of us how to give ourselves to God!" (page 103). Each day teach others, by your words and example, how we can give ourselves completely to God. "God expects something from you. Don't forget that" (pages 43 and 48).

🗓 Timeline Work
Add the dates and events from 1858 through 1907 to complete your timeline.

Dedication of the Days of the Week and Months of the Year

Although these will vary slightly depending on the source, the following lists show each day's or month's dedication. Decorate the house, recite special prayers, plan a procession, and/or perform specific actions or penances each day to honor the event or persons depicted.

Days of the Week

Sunday..The Holy Trinity

Monday ....The Holy Angels

Tuesday ....The Apostles (or The Holy Spirit)

Wednesday .... St. Joseph

Thursday ....Holy Eucharist

Friday .... The Passion

Saturday ....Our Lady

Months of the Year

January... The Holy Name of Jesus

February... The Passion of Our Lord

March .... St. Joseph

April..The Holy Eucharist

May..The Blessed Virgin Mary

June..The Sacred Heart of Jesus

July.. The Most Precious Blood

August .... The Immaculate Heart of Mary

September .... Our Lady of Sorrows

October...The Most Holy Rosary

November.................... The Holy Souls Detained in Purgatory

December ....The Divine Infancy

✎ Book Summary Test for *The Miraculous Medal*

Directions: Answer in complete sentences. If necessary, use the back of the page for additional writing space. 100 possible points, 20 points for each answer.

1. In St. Catherine's childhood dreams, who kept beckoning to her? What were the words he used to call her?

   _____

   _____

2. At what age did Catherine enter the religious order of the Daughters of Charity? How long had she waited to become a religious? Why had she waited?

   _____

   _____

3. What were St. Catherine's duties at the convent of the Daughters of Charity?

   _____

   _____

4. Other than the Miraculous Medal, what else did our Lady request St. Catherine to make? Describe the image of the Miraculous Medal. What is its most important aspect?

   _____

   _____

   _____

5. St. Catherine describes children as "tools in His service" (page 104). What role did she feel children played in promoting the devotion to the Miraculous Medal and teaching others about giving ourselves to God? What can you do to promote the devotion to the Miraculous Medal?

   _____

   _____

   _____

The Miraculous Medal, The Story of Our Lady's Appearances to Saint Catherine Labouré

Answer Key to Comprehension Questions

Chapters 1 through 3—In Which the Blessed Virgin Appears to Sister Labouré and Gives Her a Special Mission

1. Sister Labouré was awakened around midnight on the night of July 18, 1830, by a little boy who asked her to accompany him to the chapel where he said the Blessed Virgin awaited her.
2. Sister Labouré later told Father Aladel that she believed that the little boy was her guardian angel.
3. In November, Sister Labouré heard a heavenly voice that spoke within the depths of her own heart telling her to have a medal made after the model of her vision (page 15).
4. Sister Labouré was asked to have a medal made in honor of the Blessed Virgin Mary. The medal was to be modeled after the image that Sister Labouré saw on November 27, 1830, when our Lady appeared holding a globe representing the world surmounted with a cross. The front of the medal was to be a picture of the Blessed Virgin with rays of grace descending from her hands. An oval frame surrounded the Blessed Virgin with an inscription in golden letters: "O Mary, conceived without sin, pray for us who have recourse to thee." On the back of the medal was to be the letter "M" surmounted by a cross and a bar. Beneath the "M" were to be the hearts of Jesus and Mary. Twelve stars were to encircle the back image.

Chapters 4 through 6—In Which Sister Labouré Receives the Habit of a Daughter of Charity, and the Bishop Agrees to Begin Work on the Medal

1. Sister Labouré was directed to place the words "O Mary, conceived without sin, pray for us who have recourse to thee" on the medal.
2. In January of 1831, Sister Labouré received the habit of a Daughter of Charity of St. Vincent de Paul (also known as the "Sisters of Charity") and assumed the name of Sister Catherine. The order of the Daughters of Charity is dedicated to the special work of caring for the poor and sick.
3. Father Aladel decided to see the Archbishop about the medal as proposed by Sister Catherine when she quoted the words of the Blessed Virgin to him: "Don't worry. A day will come when Father Aladel will do what I wish. He is my servant, and would fear to displease me" (page 25).

Chapters 7 through 9—In Which the Medal Is Made, Distributed, and Named "Miraculous"

1. The rays extending from our Lady's hands on the medal represent every kind of blessing that our Lady wants to give us.
2. The stipulations for acquiring the great graces that abound from the medal include wearing the medal from the neck, having the medal blessed before wearing, and wearing it with confidence.
3. The adjective "Miraculous" become attached to this medal after it was observed how the medal preserved its wearers from the cholera plague, even curing those on the verge of death.
4. Catherine asked the Blessed Virgin to be her mother when she was nine years old, immediately after her own mother died. (A few years later, Catherine's father entrusted her with the care of the other nine Labouré children as well as the household.) Mary took care of Catherine by seeing to it that the neighbors were very kind, looking after her brothers, and interceding with Catherine's Aunt Marguerite so she was inspired to take Catherine and her little sister in to live with her.

Chapters 10 through 12—In Which Old John Is Converted, and Sister Catherine Shows Father Aladel a Pathway to Heaven
1. The priest of Catherine's dreams was St. Vincent de Paul, the founder of the Daughters of Charity.
2. Twelve years of suffering and prayer prepared Catherine to enter the convent of the Daughters of Charity.
3. To help bring about the conversion of John, Sister Catherine not only prayed for him (especially at Mass) but also worked without complaining, never asked for privileges, kneeled for prayer instead of sitting, and fasted on various days. She placed John in our Lady's hands.

Chapters 13 through 15—In Which the Medal Lives Up to Its Name, and The Association of the Children of Mary Is Founded
1. In Chapter 13 John expresses a desire to make a good confession to a priest and, in thanksgiving, to attempt to get other men interested in wearing the Miraculous Medal.
2. Catherine's assistance in the conversion of John helped convince the sisters at Enghien that Sister Catherine was the nun responsible for the Miraculous Medal. However, when she left her work in the kitchen for duties in the laundry and linen room, they decided she could not be the sister who saw the Blessed Virgin.
3. In order to be blessed with rich indulgences, the Children of Mary wished to become affiliated with the Jesuit society of *La Prima Primaria*, a society of students established in 1534 whose primary purpose was to honor the Mother of God.

Chapters 16 through 18—In Which War Causes the Daughters of Charity to Leave Enghien, and Our Lady Makes a New Request
1. The aspect of the Miraculous Medal that was the most special to Sister Catherine was the "rays of glory" (pages 76). She viewed our Lady's hands as "the source of all grace for suffering mankind" (page 77).
2. The three duties of Sister Catherine at the convent at Enghien included work in the kitchen, then work in the laundry and linen room, and later the charge of the older men housed at Enghien. (In Chapter 18 her duty of caring for the poultry yard is also mentioned.)
3. The Daughters of Charity were forced to leave the Enghien convent in April of 1871 due to a rebellion in Paris against the French government.
4. Around 1871, our Lady made a new request of Catherine. She asked Catherine to make a statue representing our Lady's appearance to Catherine on November 27, 1830, in which she appeared holding a golden globe—the world—to her heart. As Father Aladel was no longer living, Catherine was unable to fulfill this request. The strain of not obeying our Lady's wishes became so great that Catherine's health began to fail.

Chapters 19 through 21—In Which Catherine Fulfills Our Lady's Request and Dies in Peace
1. Sister Catherine, who was in ill health, made the uncomfortable trip to Paris to see the convent's confessor, Father Chinchon, as she wished to speak to him about our Lady's request that a statue be made.
2. As Catherine was unable to see Father Chinchon, she finally decided to confide in her mother superior. After revealing herself as the sister of Miraculous Medal, she related our Lady's request for a new statue.
3. Sister Catherine had kept secret her role as the sister of the Miraculous Medal for forty-six years.
4. Sister Catherine was disappointed in the statue because, although it was beautiful, it did not begin to capture the true beauty our Lady and fell far short of resembling her. (Note that in 1934 St. Faustina guided an artist to draw an image of the Divine Mercy of Jesus as He had appeared to her. As recorded in her diary, *Divine Mercy in My* Soul, she was disappointed at the artist's rendition and cried to the Lord, "Who will paint You as beautiful as You are?" He

replied, "Not in the beauty of the color, nor of the brush lies the greatness of this image, but in My grace" (*Diary*, 313).

5. The example of Catherine's humble life revealed to others the truth about holiness—it "is not so much a matter of long prayers and great sacrifices as it is of giving oneself completely into God's hands for Him to do with as He wills" (page 103). Her life made others realize that the secret of being a saint was "first to give themselves to God *completely*. . . . then wait in loving confidence for Him to make known His Will" (page 103). St. Catherine felt that children can best "teach the rest of us how to give ourselves to God" (page 103).

Answer Key to Book Summary Test

1. In St. Catherine's childhood dreams, an old priest, whom she later identified as St. Vincent de Paul, beckoned to her, calling, "My child, you avoid me just now, but a day will come when you will seek me out. God expects something from you. Don't forget that" (pages 43 and 48).

2. St. Catherine entered the religious order of the Daughters of Charity at the age of twenty-four, after having prepared for twelve years by prayer and suffering. Although St. Catherine felt that her entrance into the Daughters of Charity was God's will for her, her father was opposed to Catherine's religious vocation even though she had expressed it to him since she was twelve.

3. Catherine's humble duties at the convent at Enghien included working in the kitchen, and then working in the laundry and linen room. Later she was put in charge of the older men housed at Enghien as well the poultry yard.

4. Other than the Miraculous Medal, our Lady requested that St. Catherine facilitate in the sculpturing of a statue made in the image of our Lady as she appeared to St. Catherine on November 20, 1830—holding a golden globe, representing the world, to her heart. The front of the medal bears the image of the Blessed Virgin with her fingers sending out rays and the words, "O Mary, conceived without sin, pray for us who have recourse to thee" inscribed in a horseshoe shape over the image. The back of the medal has the letter "M" with a cross and bar on top with two hearts—one with thorns and the other pierced by a sword—below it. Twelve stars surround the outer border. The most important aspect of the medal is the rays extending from our Lady's hands as they represent every kind of blessing that our Lady wishes to give us.

5. St. Catherine believed that children best know how to give themselves completely to God. They are not afraid of what He may ask them to do (pages 103-106). Answers to the second question will vary.

Other RACE for Heaven Products

Catholic Study Guides for Mary Fabyan Windeatt's Saint Biography Series teach the Catholic faith to all members of your family. Written with your family's various learning levels in mind, these flexible study guides succeed as stand-alone unit studies or supplements to your regular curriculum. Thirty to sixty minutes per day will allow your family to experience:

- ☑ The spirituality and holy habits of the saints
- ☑ Lively family discussions on important faith topics
- ☑ Increased critical thinking and reading comprehension skills
- ☑ Quality read-aloud time with Catholic "living books"
- ☑ Enhanced knowledge of Catholic doctrine and the Bible
- ☑ History and geography incorporated into saintly literature
- ☑ Writing projects based on secular and Catholic historical events and characters

Purchase these guides individually or in the following grade-level packages. (Grade level is are determined solely on the length of each book in the series.)

Grades 3-4: *St. Thomas Aquinas, The Story of the "Dumb Ox"; St. Catherine of Siena, The Girl Who Saw Saints in the Sky; Patron Saint of First Communicants, The Story of Blessed Imelda Lambertini;* and *The Miraculous Medal, The Story of Our Lady's Appearances to St. Catherine Labouré*

Grade 5: *St. Rose, First Canonized Saint of the Americas; St. Martin de Porres, The Story of the Little Doctor of Lima, Peru; King David and His Songs, A Story of the Psalms;* and *Blessed Marie of New France, The Story of the First Missionary Sisters in Canada*

Grade 6: *St. Dominic, Preacher of the Rosary and Founder of the Dominicans; St. Benedict, The Story of the Father of the Western Monks; The Children of Fatima and Our Lady's Message to the World;* and *St. John Masias, Marvelous Dominican Gate-keeper of Lima, Peru*

Grade 7: *The Little Flower, The Story of St. Therese of the Child Jesus; St. Hyacinth, The Story of the Apostle of the North; The Curé of Ars, The Story of St. John Vianney, Patron Saint of Parish Priests;* and *St. Louis de Montfort, The Story of Our Lady's Slave*

Grade 8: *Pauline Jaricot, Foundress of the Living Rosary and the Society for the Propagation of Faith; St. Francis Solano, Wonder-Worker of the New World and Apostle of Argentina and Peru; St. Paul the Apostle, The Story of the Apostle to the Gentiles;* and *St. Margaret Mary, Apostle of the Sacred Heart*

The Windeatt Dictionary: Pre-Vatican II Terms and Catholic Words from Mary Fabyan Windeatt's Saint Biographies explains over 450 Catholic terms and expressions used in this popular saint biography series. Indispensable in expanding knowledge and practice of the Catholic faith, this book provides a ready access for the Catholic vocabulary words used in the RACE for Heaven Windeatt study guides. This dictionary also includes a Catholic book report resource that contains suggestions for forty-five Catholic book reports: fourteen writing projects, ten book report activities, and twenty-one topics for saint biographies.

Graced Encounters with Mary Fabyan Windeatt's Saints: 344 Ways to Imitate the Holy Habits of the Saints is a compilation of the "Growing in Holiness" sections of RACE for Heaven's Catholic study guides for the Windeatt saint biography series and presents 344 examples of saintly behavior, one for nearly every chapter in each of these twenty biographies. Enhance your encounter with the saints by practicing the models of devotion, service, penance, prayer, and virtue offered in this guide.

Bedtime Bible Stories for Catholic Children: Loving Jesus through His Word contains twenty discussions of Bible stories that were originally published in serial form in a Catholic children's magazine. Their author stated, "The tales are extremely simple and unadorned. They are real conversations of a real child and her mother." Due to popular demand, the series was later (1910) published as a book, *Bible Stories Told to "Toddles."* The engaging conversational style of this book lends itself well as a bedtime read-aloud that allows Jesus to come alive in the Gospels. The study aids include discussion questions to help foster spiritual conversation, Bible excerpts relevant to the presented story, "Growing in Holiness" suggestions for living the Gospel message in our daily lives, and short catechism lessons for both children and adults.

I Talk with God: The Art of Prayer and Meditation for Catholic Children strives to instill in young Catholics a love of prayer and a practical knowledge of the art of meditation. This prayer book contains prayers to pray out loud (vocal prayer) or in the silence of your heart. It shows how you can talk with God, and more importantly, how you can love God. As you progress through this book—from discovering what prayer is to reading and reciting simple prayers to understanding meditation and then to helps for deeper meditation—you will see that prayer and meditation often go together. Meditation is described by the big *Catechism of the Catholic Church* as nothing more than "prayerful reflection" or *holy thinking.* You can use books, devotions, pictures, holy cards, and images (such as the stained glass windows in church) to help you think about holy people, events, and ideas. Learn how to talk with God each day to increase your love for Him and follow more closely His holy will.

Communion with the Saints: A Family Preparation Program for First Communion and Beyond in the Spirit of St. Therese imitates St. Therese of the Child Jesus and her family who studied and prayed for sixty-nine days in anticipation of Therese's First Holy Communion. Modeling this preparation, the *Communion with the Saints* program will help any family find renewed fervor in the reception of the Eucharist. This resource includes a chapter-by-chapter study of the following four books:

- *The Little Flower, The Story of Saint Therese of the Child Jesus*—to provide the foundation of God's love for us and to encourage a desire for holiness

- *The Children of Fatima and Our Lady's Message to the World*—to show the sinfulness of our world and the need to avoid sin

- *The Patron Saint of First Communicants, The Story of Blessed Imelda Lambertini*—to inspire devotion to the Sacrament of Holy Communion

- *The King of the Golden City* by Mother Mary Loyola —to illustrate Jesus' Presence as a source of grace necessary to live a holy life

Each of the sixty-nine days of preparation includes read-aloud selections with enrichment activities, meditational readings, catechism lessons, and plenty of practical application to promote a growth in holiness and sanctity. Weekend suggestions include a list of over thirty-five family projects. The use of *My First Communion Journal* is encouraged with this program.

My First Communion Journal in Imitation of Saint Therese, The Little Flower provides a lasting keepsake of a child's First Holy Communion. This journal has been constructed in imitation of the copybook made for Therese Martin by her older sister Pauline to help Therese prepare for her First Holy Communion. Although this book is not an exact replica of the copybook used by Therese, it does contain many of the same prayers and aspirations she used, the same idea of flowers inspiring virtue, and the same method of recording prayers recited and sacrifices made. It is up to you to decorate and complete this journal, replicating Therese's heroic efforts by raising your mind and heart to Jesus and by humbling yourself with small sacrifices. Learn as well to imitate St. Therese's love and knowledge of Scripture as you meditate on—or even memorize—the biblical passages that are provided for reflection. This journal may be completed in conjunction with the *Communion with the Saints* program or used separately.

My First Communion Journal in Imitation of St. Paul, Putting on the Armor of God was also inspired by St. Therese's copybook and uses the same method of encouraging—and recording—daily prayers and mortifications. However, instead of using flowers to illustrate virtues, this resource uses the battle model St. Paul describes in Ephesians 6:10-17. First communicants are encouraged to arm themselves with virtues and spiritual weapons in order to fight as soldiers of Christ. The scriptural words of Jesus and St. Paul are reflected on frequently to encourage the imitation of the actions and love of Jesus and to inspire a love and knowledge of Holy Scripture. This journal too may be completed in conjunction with the *Communion with the Saints* program or used separately.

The King of the Golden City Study Edition is a new edition of a book that was originally published in 1921. This treasure of a book was written in response to a student's appeal for instructions along with "little stories" to help her prepare for Holy Communion. To fulfill this request, Mother Loyola of the Bar Convent in York, England, wrote a simple story that illustrates Jesus' desire to share an intimate relationship with each one of His children. This new edition contains some updated language but, quite deliberately, does not contain any pictures. Readers, as they progress through this story, will form a mental image of their King, one as unique and personal as their own relationship with Him. The study sections assist with the allegory, connect to the Bible as well as to the catechism, and explore the art of prayer in the spirit of the three Carmelite Doctors of the Church. Although written over ninety years ago for a young child, this book remains a timeless masterpiece of Catholic literature suitable for all ages. (Also available as a study guide only)

The Good Shepherd and His Little Lambs Study Edition is a simply told Catholic tale of four children who meet with their beloved aunt for "First Communion talks." More than a story, it is a First Communion primer that takes the tenets of the catechism and, through naturally-flowing conversations, relates them in the language of little ones to authentic Christian living. As Mrs. Bosch explains, "We might learn the catechism all the way through beautifully, and at the end find ourselves still very stiff and clumsy about loving our Lord. When He comes to us, we don't want to welcome Him into our souls only with answers out of the catechism, do we?" Enriched by appropriate Biblical passages, points of doctrine, and prayers, this story-primer is an enjoyable and effective read-aloud that will prepare the Good Shepherd's little lambs to worthily receive Him in the Holy Eucharist.

A Reconciliation Reader-Retreat: Read-Aloud Lessons, Stories, and Poems for Young Catholics Preparing for Confession provides a basic doctrinal explanation and review of the Sacrament of Reconciliation as well as a Gospel examination of conscience—a seven-day read-aloud formation retreat. To help the lessons come alive and to enable young Catholics to more readily apply these doctrines to their own daily lives, the lessons have been supplemented with pertinent short stories and poems. Each lesson contains reflection questions, a family prayer, and a "Gospel Examination of Conscience" that is formulated according to the dictates of the *Catechism of the Catholic Church*. This reader-retreat will not only enrich and deepen the sacramental experience for each member of your family but it will also provide several tools to help you recommit to leading a virtuous life and to grow together in holiness.

Devotion to St. Joseph: Read-Aloud Stories, Poems, and Prayers for Catholic Children encourages children to love Jesus as St. Joseph did. As Scripture does not record a single word this great saint spoke; we must take our lessons of his life from his actions. In this compilation of stories and poems about our Savior's foster-father from renowned Catholics, children of all ages are encouraged to imitate the virtues the life of St. Joseph reveal to us in his loving dedication to Jesus and Mary. The discussion questions as well as the reflections on the virtues of St. Joseph lead children to apply the lessons of this saint's life to their own while the prayer section promotes a lasting devotion to the great St. Joseph. As St. Teresa of Avila declared, "I wish I could persuade everyone to be devoted to this glorious saint!"

The Month of St. Joseph: Prayers and Practices for Each Day of March in Imitation of the Virtues of St. Joseph was originally published in 1874. This book contains daily meditations on the life and virtues of St. Joseph for adults and high-school students. In addition, each day presents a prayer to St. Joseph, several resolutions, a short ejaculatory prayer, a relevant Scripture verse, and a brief consideration for reflection. The practices for each day are intended to assist the reader in acquiring the habits of prayer and interior recollection so necessary to living in the presence of God. Perfect for Lenten reading, this journey through the life of St. Joseph reveals his love of God and neighbor, humility, quiet action, and spirit of sacrifice. While the Bible tells so little about St. Joseph's life, here we discover the abundant virtues of this silent saint—and are challenged to imitate them.

Alternative Book Reports for Catholic Students contains forty-five book report ideas to encourage critical thinking for ages seven to fourteen. These ideas are intended to provoke a reflection on those themes and topics that support and encourage Catholic living as well as some that may conflict with our Faith. Many report topics require an examination of our personal faith life and prompt us to take lessons from the saints to strengthen our own faith in God. The suggested activities vary from written exercises to creative art projects and include twenty-one topics specifically designed for saint biographies. Other activities can be used within a group or family.

Reading the Saints: Lists of Catholic Books for Children Plus Book Collecting Tips for the Home and School Library (formerly entitled *Saintly Resources*) is a valuable tool for Catholic home educators, classroom teachers, and collectors of Catholic juvenile books. This resource will help you discover living books from such popular out-of-print Catholic juvenile series as Catholic Treasury, Vision Books, and American Background Books as well as current series books for young Catholics. Use this book to find:

- Over 800 Catholic books listed by author, series, reading level, century, and geographical location
- More than 275 authors of saint biographies, historical fiction, and poetry written for Catholic juvenile readers
- Publishers of Catholic children's books, present and past
- Helpful advice for collecting and caring for used books
- Hundreds of age-appropriate, accessible living books to enrich your study of the Catholic Church's rich heritage of saints and notable Catholic historical figures
- Information on how to build and maintain your own library of Catholic juvenile books
- Inspiring quotations about book collecting, reading, and the love of books

The Outlaws of Ravenhurst Study Edition contains a classic story of the persecution of Scottish Catholics that was first written in 1923 and was revised and reprinted in 1950. This 2009 edition of Sr. M. Imelda Wallace's *Outlaws of Ravenhurst* contains the revised story of 1950 plus chapter-by-chapter aids to assist readers in assimilating the book's strong Catholic elements into their own lives. The study section focuses on critical thinking, integration of biblical teachings, and the study of the virtuous life to which Christ calls us as mature Catholics. With its emphasis on virtues (theological and moral plus the gifts and fruits of the Holy Spirit), the spiritual and corporal works of mercy, and the Beatitudes, *Outlaws of Ravenhurst Study Edition* is a fun and effective catechetical tool for Catholics preparing for the Sacrament of Confirmation. (Also available as a study guide only)

The Family that Overtook Christ Study Edition: The Story of the Family of St. Bernard of Clairvaux is an excellent read for young adults who are preparing to receive the Sacrament of Confirmation. In this exciting chronicle of the life of twelfth-century knights, we have an entire family of nine saints who lay before us their individual means of achieving intimate union with Christ. Learn with the Fontaines family how to supernaturalize the natural, develop a God-consciousness, and attain sanctity by being yourself. Perfect for high-school read-aloud (or adult study), this new study edition has over 250 footnotes for increased comprehension and provides discussion/meditation points to promote the art of spiritual conversation. The appendix lists formulas of Catholic doctrine that are essential for confirmands not only to know but also to incorporate into their own spiritual lives.

A Confirmation Reader-Retreat: Read-Aloud Lessons, Stories and Poems for Young Catholics utilizes chapters from two excellent out-of-print Catholic books for children (*I Belong to God, Great Truths in Simple Stories for Children and Lovers of Children* by Lillian Clark; and *Children's Retreats in Preparation for First Confession, First Holy Communion, and Confirmation* by Rev. P.A. Halpin). This book provides a basic doctrinal review of the Sacrament of Confirmation as well as prayer experiences—a nine-day read-aloud retreat/novena. The reprinted material has been supplemented with short stories and poems that provide insights in applying catechetical doctrines to the daily life of young Catholics. Each lesson concludes with "I Talk with God"—a section that encourages readers (of all ages) to deepen their relationship with each of the Three Persons of the Blessed Trinity. Reflection questions promote the habit of spiritual conversation within your family—to encourage family members to discuss holy topics—and to help you grow together in holiness. Additionally, a traditional novena to the Holy Spirit is included.

By Cross and Anchor Study Edition: The Story of Frederic Baraga on Lake Superior relates the exciting, and often miraculous, missionary adventures of the "Snowshoe Priest"—Venerable Frederic Baraga, the first bishop of Michigan's Upper Peninsula. Declared "Venerable" by Pope Benedict XVI on May 10, 2012, this priest came to the United States from Slovenia in 1830 to undertake his mission as a "simple servant of God." For almost forty years, Fr. Frederic Baraga traveled across over 80,000 square miles of wilderness by snowshoe in winter and canoe in summer. In imitation of Christ, Bishop Baraga become poor so that he might bring the riches of the Catholic Faith to the Chippewa and immigrant residents of the beautiful peninsula he served. Although not strictly a biography, this book is a story based on historical facts drawn from Bishop Baraga's own journal and letters—a fascinating, easy-to-read history of Michigan's northern peninsula. While this exciting adventure is intended for youth who are interested in knowing more about this quiet, courageous priest, readers of all ages will be inspired by his life of humility, simplicity, and selfless virtue. This new study edition contains over 130 footnotes, defining less familiar vocabulary words and—gleaned from Venerable Baraga's *Journal* and other primary sources—details regarding the region's people and places. Also included are discussion questions, applicable Scripture passages, pertinent quotations of Venerable Baraga from the text, and—most importantly—a section illustrating how to imitate the various virtues of Venerable Frederic Baraga. Additionally, the complete text of Bishop Baraga's 1853 "Pastoral Letter to the Faithful" has been included with numerous references added in order that we may read this in light of Scripture and the *Compendium of the Catechism of the Catholic Church*. Learn more about the life, ministry, and heroic virtues of Venerable Frederic Baraga, the "Snowshoe Priest."

To Order: Email info@RACEforHeaven.com or place an order at RACEforHeaven.com. Discover, MasterCard, VISA, PayPal, American Express, checks, and money orders are accepted.

www.ingramcontent.com/pod-product-compliance
Lightning Source LLC
Chambersburg PA
CBHW081106270725
30205CB00036B/528